CLUEDLE

THE CASE OF THE
GOLDEN POMEGRANATE

Also available:

Cluedle: The Case of the Dumpleton Diamond

Coming soon:

Cluedle: The Case of Rudolph's Revenge

CLUEDLE

THE CASE OF THE GOLDEN POMEGRANATE

HARTIGAN BROWNE

WORKMAN PUBLISHING • NEW YORK

Copyright © 2024 by Hartigan Browne

Workman Kids
Workman Publishing
Hachette Book Group, Inc.
1290 Avenue of the Americas
New York, NY 10104
workman.com

Workman Kids is an imprint of Workman Publishing, a division of Hachette Book Group, Inc. The Workman name and logo are registered trademarks of Hachette Book Group, Inc.

Design by Daniella Graner and Jennifer Keenan
Photo credits: Shutterstock

The publisher is not responsible for websites (or their content) that are not owned by the publisher.

Workman books may be purchased in bulk for business, educational, or promotional use. For information, please contact your local bookseller or the Hachette Book Group Special Markets Department at special.markets@hbgusa.com.

ISBN 978-1-5235-3167-7

Ebook ISBNs 978-1-5235-3200-1, 978-1-5235-3201-8, 978-1-5235-3202-5
First Edition October 2024 VER

Originally published in the UK by Macmillan Children's Books, an imprint of Pan Macmillan, in 2024.

Printed in Illinois, USA, on responsibly sourced paper.

10 9 8 7 6 5 4 3 2 1

[HARTIGAN BROWNE'S] CASE FILE

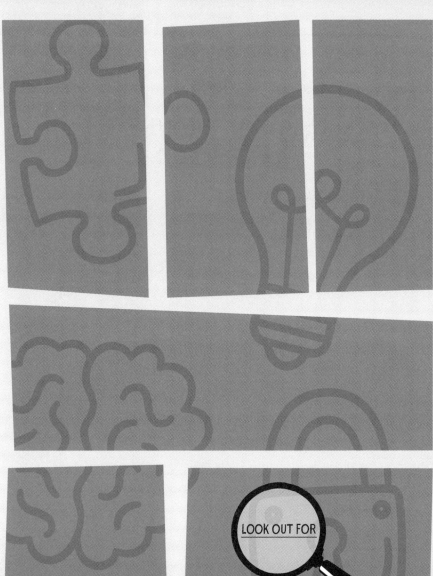

LOOK OUT FOR

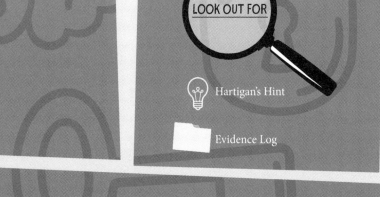

Hartigan's Hint

Evidence Log

AGENT SELECTION

Hello there, young detective, it's Hartigan Browne. I trust this message finds you well and still of brilliant mind and courageous countenance because I have a new case for you to investigate.

How are your sea legs? I do hope they're sturdy because you're about to set sail on a luxury superyacht. But don't get too excited; this won't be all rainbows and lollipops, for you have a crime to solve. I see your curiosity is piqued: Could it be a robbery, a poisoning, a spot of blackmail, or perhaps all three? Take a look at the case outline and find out.

For security, the file is passcode protected and for your eyes only. Once you have opened it, we'll begin your briefing. This should get you back into the swing of things!

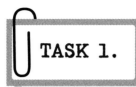

TASK 1.

The case outline is protected by a four-digit passcode, which can be determined by finding the number code for the word OPEN.

The words and number codes below will lead you to the answer.

This may look tricky at first glance, but as you well know, appearances can often be deceptive. There is a logical solution and I know you can find it!

TONE	PENT	NOTE
8123	2183	5328

You have not been told which code applies to which word. Can you work out through your tremendous powers of deduction which numbers match with which letters?

Compare the position of the numbers to the letters in the words. You can work out that the number 3 represents the letter E because two of the codes have a 3 in the final position and NOTE and TONE both have the letter E in the final position.

8	1	2	3
2	1	8	3
5	3	2	8

The number code for OPEN is: _ _ _ _

 HARTIGAN'S HINT: Have a look at those numbers. You can start by working out what letter the number 1 represents. It is found in the second position in *two* of the words. What is it?

Answer on page 180

Input the four-digit code for OPEN here:

Are you in? I do believe you are! Bravo, detective!

Answer on page 182

Here's the case outline:

Alotta Vibrato, retired international opera singer.

Alotta is currently on an expedition to find the missing notes from the world-famous opera *The Pegasus*. *The Pegasus*, composer unknown, is considered to be the most beautiful piece of music ever created by humankind and is based on music written by the ancient Greeks. While some believe the work was never finished, others assert that it still exists; however, searches for the final pages of the sheet music have been unsuccessful. Alotta has recently discovered a clue to their whereabouts. She has invited a select group of friends and acquaintances to join her on her luxury yacht to assist in her quest.

However, the clue that she had to the sheet music's location has vanished. She believes one of her guests has stolen it, and she needs *you* to discover who. Find the clue, and then the music, so Alotta can mark her comeback with the world's first performance of *The Pegasus* in its entirety.

Alotta has gone to great lengths to keep the ship's location a secret in order to prevent reporters and the paparazzi discovering her whereabouts. To determine the location of the *Icarus Infinity*, you will have to decipher the following code.

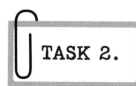

TASK 2.

Use the table below to solve the equations, right, that reveal the coordinates of the *Icarus Infinity*.

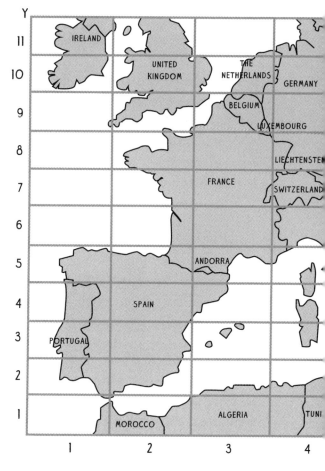

Notes:

The coordinates of the *Icarus Infinity* are:

X = _____   Y = _____

Where are you headed?

_____

X	Y
$(\eta-\gamma)+\alpha$	$\dfrac{\theta}{\gamma}$ or $\theta \div \gamma$

1	2	3	4	5	6	7	8	9
α	β	γ	δ	ε	ς	ζ	η	θ

 HARTIGAN'S HINT: This may look terribly complicated, but it is simply a case of replacing the Greek symbols with the corresponding numbers. Calculate the equation in the parentheses first!

Answer on page 183

I knew you'd solve it! Now, time is a-wasting and you have some investigating to do. First, you're going to need a plane ticket ...

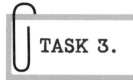

TASK 3.

To print your ticket, select the correct final arrow button in the sequence below.

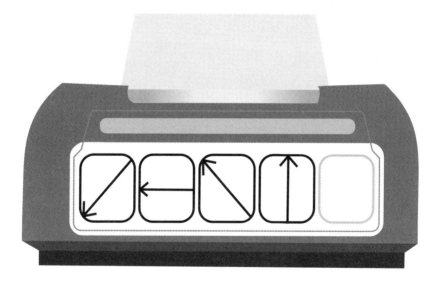

 HARTIGAN'S HINT:
The arrows are
rotating clockwise.

Circle the letter of the button that completes the sequence.

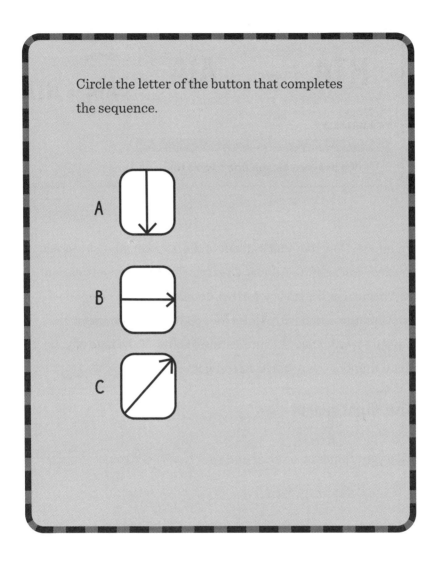

Answer on page 184

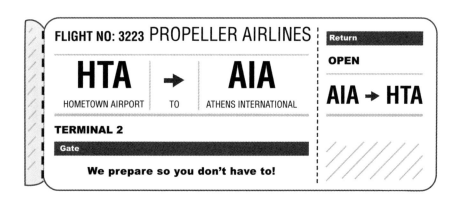

FLIGHT NO: 3223 PROPELLER AIRLINES

HTA ➡ **AIA**

HOMETOWN AIRPORT | TO | ATHENS INTERNATIONAL

TERMINAL 2

Gate

We prepare so you don't have to!

Return

OPEN

AIA ➡ HTA

Fabulous! Now that that's all out of the way, get your sunscreen packed. You're off to Athens, Greece, where your investigation will begin. I will send you further details about the telephone conversation I had with Alotta for you to review on the plane. I'm sure it will make for interesting reading. Take note of your flight number—you will be needing it.

The flight number is: _ _ _ _

May your thoughts be clear and your theories strong!

Answer on page 184

Who:

Where:

What:

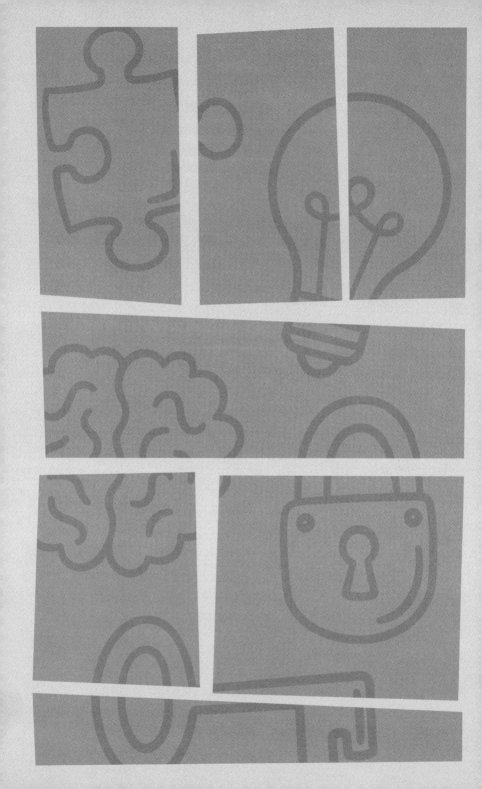

CASE 1:

AHOY THERE, SUSPECTS!

You're buckled into your seat on a flight to Athens when a flight attendant hands you a tray of plane food. You're about to peel the foil off a dish claiming to be lamb moussaka when you spot something else on the tray. It's a computer tablet, and you correctly deduce that it contains further notes on your case. I have also included a recording of me playing Handel's Oboe Sonata in C minor to keep you entertained during the flight. You are most welcome.

The case notes are, of course, passcode protected. You can never be too careful with airlines. I once failed to lock my suitcase and all my clothes ended up strewn across the runway. I had to spend a week in Rome sporting very substandard undergarments. Anyway, I digress.

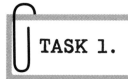

TASK 1.

To unlock the tablet, you will need to press the correct four numbers in order in the grid.

You were told to remember a number before you left on this mission. Each digit represents the number of spaces you must move in the direction of each arrow. The space you land on at the end of each move will, in sequence, reveal a new four-digit code.

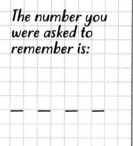

The number you were asked to remember is:

_ _ _ _

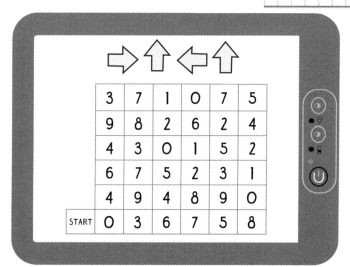

Write your answer here: _ _ _ _

 HARTIGAN'S HINT: The number will be just the *ticket* to solving this! The arrows show you the direction you must move. The square you land on after each movement is a number in the tablet code.

Answer on page 185

Excellent! Now that you've unlocked the tablet, you can access the details from the phone call I had with Alotta Vibrato when she phoned me from the *Icarus Infinity* to request our services:

I was tootling merrily away on my oboe when the phone rang. I put my instrument aside and my brow twitched — a sure sign that a mystery was afoot.

The voice on the end of the phone was curt and to the point.

"Someone has stolen something from me, and I would very much like you to get it back."

"Who is this? And what is it that has been stolen?" I inquired.

Alotta introduced herself and told me about the clue leading to the missing song notes of *The Pegasus*.

I admit, I gasped. "I thought the missing music was a myth!" I said, trying hard to maintain my composure.

"My dear friend and composer Sascha van Tootahonk did not think so. He searched for it until the day he died. He insisted he had a clue to its whereabouts, but he was never able to locate it. On his deathbed, he left the clue to me, saying his dying wish was that I should one day find the music and perform *The Pegasus* in its entirety. 'Sail to Greece, my muse, and find it,' he said. I promised him I would."

"My goodness," I said. "*The Pegasus*! That would be incredible. Did you crack the clue?"

(continued)

(continued)

"No, I didn't, and it will be very difficult for me to do so now that I don't have it. I invited some guests aboard my yacht, either to assist with the search or to document it. I believe one of them is the culprit."

"I'll need a list of names."

Alotta agreed to send them over, then said, "It is incredibly important that the missing song notes are found. I have come out of retirement to sing *The Pegasus*. The world's eyes will be on me, and I've promised them something their ears have never heard before."

I told her I understood and that I had an agent I could send right away. Alotta hung up and moments later I received an email with the list of the people aboard the *Icarus Infinity*.

So here you are, jetting off to Greece. Let's get you up to speed. Because the clue was stolen when the ship was at sea, these are your prime suspects:

CAPTAIN HARALAMBOS HONDROS

RELEVANCE: Captain of the *Icarus Infinity*

A seasoned explorer, discovered treasures such as the Merman's Emerald Eyeball and Nefertiti's Golde Kneecap in his younger years.

TELLY PAPAS

RELEVANCE: Ship steward

Aboard the *Icarus Infinity* to provide the highest standard of care to the owner and guests.

IVOR PENN

RELEVANCE: Journalist and critic

On board to review Alotta's performance and write an article about it for *The Daily Wail* newspaper.

PROFESSOR ARCHIBALD RANGLEFOOT

RELEVANCE: World-renowned historian

Good friend to Alotta. As a historian, has a particular interest in Greek history.

MAY WAIL

RELEVANCE: Alotta's much younger stepsister

Trying to make it as a singer on the opera scene. Married to Will Wail.

WILL WAIL

RELEVANCE: Owns *The Daily Wail* newspaper

Very supportive of his new wife's career.

HILARIA SCRIBBLES

RELEVANCE: Author

Employed by Alotta to write her biography. Thrilled to have a trip to Greece entirely compensated.

ANITA SLEEP

RELEVANCE: Personal Assistant

Has worked for Alotta Vibrato for three years without a pay raise.

That makes eight suspects. It's up to you to find out who is responsible for stealing the clue.

When you arrive at Athens International Airport, a driver collects you from arrivals and escorts you to the Port of Piraeus to board the *Icarus Infinity*. You are met there by Telly Papas, the ship's steward, who takes you aboard a speedboat and straight to the *Icarus*, which is anchored in the turqoise blue of the Aegean Sea. Once aboard, Telly Papas chauffeurs you directly to Alotta's cabin.

As you start to make your way down the corridor toward Alotta's room, you immediately hear singing. She's really going for it, but the sound that she's producing isn't one that could be described as pleasant by any stretch of the imagination. As you go to knock on the door, she builds to a crescendo, missing the final note quite spectacularly.

The door is opened by an exhausted-looking woman who introduces herself as Anita Sleep.

"Uno momento!" comes a shout from behind a dressing screen. A few seconds later, Alotta Vibrato emerges in a billowing kaftan holding Sonata, her pet Chihuahua.

Anita backs out of the door and you explain to Alotta you are there to investigate the theft. You ask her if she can describe the clue that was stolen from her, and she tells you it was a scroll bearing a lot of incomprehensible shapes and lines. She had hoped to show it to the historian, Professor Ranglefoot, that morning, because of his extensive knowledge of Greek history, but it was taken before she had a chance. You ask her where the scroll was kept, and she shows you the safe in her room.

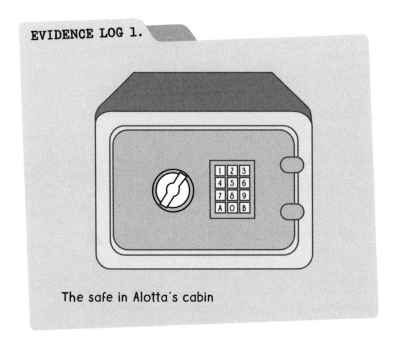

The safe in Alotta's cabin

She tells you that she didn't think anyone else knew the code and pulls out a piece of paper from her bag. "At my age, you need something to jog your memory when it comes to passwords and PIN numbers. I use musical notes to help me remember. For example, the PIN for my phone is *semiquaver, minim, crotchet,* which is 1624.

"I wonder if you can figure it out," she says. "Let's see if you're up to the job of detective."

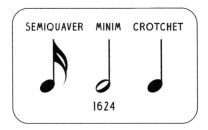

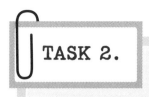

TASK 2.

The code for the safe is:

Find the pattern in the chart below and fill in the missing numbers.

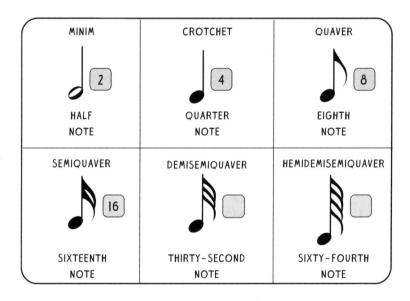

What is the four-digit PIN? _ _ _ _

You open the safe and take out a piece of very old-looking paper.

Alotta tells you that it was sent to her by Sascha van Tootahonk along with the scroll bearing the clue to the missing music. She has no idea what the paper is, or whether it is important. Whoever stole the scroll certainly didn't seem to think this paper was valuable. Or maybe they didn't see it.

You take it for evidence. It appears to be some kind of grid with a crown on top of it.

Answer on page 185

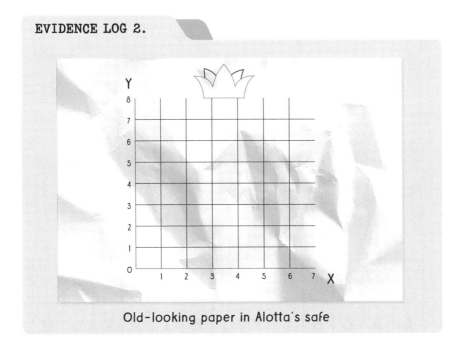

Old-looking paper in Alotta's safe

When you ask for an approximate time when the scroll was taken, Alotta tells you that it was in the safe when she left for dinner on the top deck at 7:00 p.m., but when she returned to her cabin just before 9:00 p.m., the scroll had vanished.

To get through doors in the yacht, each guest was given their own code based on the first four letters of their first name. If their name is only three letters long, their code includes the first letter of their surname.

Excellent. You may be able to narrow down your suspects already. Alotta has a list of all the codes that were punched into the door to her corridor, but the system that records which code belongs to each guest has been wiped. You will have to crack the codes to work out who was in her corridor on the evening of the robbery.

TASK 3.

Work out who entered the corridor using this keyword code. Keyword codes work by placing the keyword at the start of the alphabet. You must fill in the missing letters in the alphabet, in alphabetical order on the grid, taking care not to repeat any letters that are in the keyword.

The keyword is ICARUS.

I	C	A	R	U	S							
A	B	C	D	E	F	G	H	I	J	K	L	M

This will show you what a letter's corresponding code letter is. Alotta has told you her code for ALOT is IHLQ. Can you work out the codes of your other suspects? Make sure that you ignore titles, such as Captain and Professor!

 HARTIGAN'S HINT: **A** has already been inserted in ICA**R**US, so the first letter you need to write in the grid is **B**. Be careful not to repeat the letters found in the word ICARUS.

N	O	P	Q	R	S	T	U	V	W	X	Y	Z

Name	First 4 Letters	Code
ALOTTA VIBRATO	ALOT	IHLQ
CAPTAIN HARALAMBOS HONDROS (HARA)		
TELLY PAPAS		
IVOR PENN		
PROFESSOR ARCHIBALD RANGLEFOOT (ARCH)		
HILARIA SCRIBBLES		
ANITA SLEEP		
MAY WAIL		
WILL WAIL		

Answer on page 186

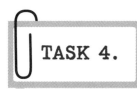

TASK 4.

Now that you have the codes, you can determine who was in the corridor in the time period that the scroll was stolen. The system records in fifteen-minute time periods. But a glitch has meant some timestamps have been lost. Recording started at 4:30 p.m. when the *Icarus Infinity* set sail and ended at 9:00 p.m. after the robbery.

Time Log for access to Alotta's corridor

Time	Codes	Suspects
4:30 P.M.	IHLQ IKEQ QUHH	
	IOAD	
	IHLQ QUHH	
	EVLO	
	JIYW	
	DIOI QUHH	
	QUHH IKEQ	

Enter the times into the correct columns in the table and then decode the codes to determine who was in the corridor during the time period of the robbery.

Time	Codes	Suspects
	IOAD DEHI	
	JIYW	
	WEHH	
	QUHH IKEQ	
7:15 P.M.		
	IKEQ	
7:45 P.M.		

Time	Codes	Suspects
	DEHI	
	IOAD QUHH	
8:30 P.M.		
	IHLQ	
9:00 P.M.	IKEQ	

Answer on page 187

Write your list of suspects here:

_____

_____

_____

_____

You decide you need to speak to these people to determine whether they had a good reason for entering the corridor around the time of the robbery.

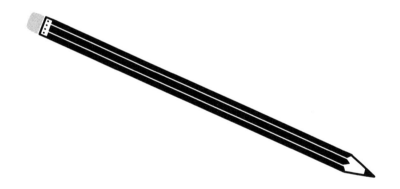

Interview notes with suspects:

ANITA SLEEP

I would never steal the scroll from Ms. Vibrato. I wouldn't dare! That evening, everyone was to meet on the top deck for a vacation-themed dinner at 7:00 p.m. I was quite out of breath from blowing up the inflatable palm trees by the time I arrived at Ms. Vibrato's room to help her dress for dinner. She needs help getting into her bottom-boosting underwear. Once I had hoisted her in, she told me she wanted to wait a while so she would be the last to arrive and make a grand entrance.

While we were waiting, Telly knocked on the door to inform her that there was a slight problem with the octopus we were supposed to be eating that evening. The problem was that he'd forgotten to actually cook it. That did not go down well with Ms. Vibrato, and she told him it better be cooked or else he'd be the one who was cooked.

When we got to the top deck, Ms. Vibrato was unhappy that her stepsister, May, wasn't already there. She and Will arrived at around 7:20 p.m. Everyone had questions about the scroll. Only Hilaria and the steward, Telly, didn't seem all that interested. Ms. Vibrato said that she would reveal the scroll the following morning. I stayed on the top deck the whole time, apart from when Ms. Vibrato sent me to her room to fetch her some peppermint tablets to aid her digestion. I don't think the octopus went down so well.

TELLY PAPAS

I was far too busy answering to Ms. Vibrato's constant stream of demands to have time to steal from her. And if I did, I would have gone for some of her fancy jewelry, not an ancient scrap of paper. I spent the whole evening serving the guests—getting this and that. Professor Ranglefoot kept going on and on asking me if there were eggs in his food because he is very allergic to them. Who would pair eggs with octopus?! Strange fellow! Hilaria Scribbles refused to eat anything that I'd cooked. She is on a special diet and showed up to dinner with a Tupperware box of her own food.

The only time I left the top deck was when I went to check on Hilaria. There'd been, how do you say . . . a freak accident involving the octopus. Ivor Penn had somehow managed to catapult a tentacle off his fork. It flew across the table with some velocity and hit Hilaria in the eye. She stormed off, and a few minutes later, Captain Haralambos sent me after her to see if she was all right. I think that must have been between 8:00 and 8:30 p.m. I found Hilaria in the corridor outside Ms. Vibrato's room. She had got herself lost — I imagine it was hard for her to see where she was going with her eye swollen up like an overripe fig.

HILARIA SCRIBBLES

I know it's unexpected that the person who wrote literary classics such as *The Potato* and *My Feet Have Toes* has agreed to pen Alotta's biography, but she offered a lot of money, and who would turn down a free cruise around the Greek Isles? Anyway, I have literally no interest in the missing music. I think it's a load of rubbish, to be honest. The evening was a total bore with everyone talking about the scroll and Alotta going on about her comeback. Her stepsister, May, didn't seem too thrilled about that. May's husband, Will, suggested Alotta and May might sing *The Pegasus* together, but that went down about as well as the octopus did.

I was in Alotta's corridor, yes, but that was by accident. That horrible little news reporter, Ivor Penn, practically blinded me with a tentacle! Honestly, it was bad enough having to sit opposite him while he chewed octopus with his mouth open. But then the tentacle missile incident happened, and I had to excuse myself. I left the table with the intention of heading to my cabin to tend to my eyeball, but I found myself quite turned around. The steward, Telly—I think—found me and helped me back to my room.

PROFESSOR ARCHIBALD RANGLEFOOT

When my dear friend Alotta invited me on this cruise and told me that she was searching for the missing music from *The Pegasus*, I must say, something stirred within me. An excitement I hadn't felt in years. That excitement diminished somewhat when I learned that Alotta is planning a comeback performance. I hope I am not being too indiscreet when I say that there was a reason she retired. A good reason. The poor old girl has quite lost it, I'm afraid. I would liken the sound she now produces to that of a goose playing the bagpipes. I fear her reputation might never recover if the public were to discover what has become of her voice. And to think that she intends to sing *The Pegasus* in its complete form! A piece of music as important and as beautiful as that does not deserve to be butchered by someone who can no longer carry a tune even if it had handles. I rather got the impression May Wail thought so, too.

But still, the music must be found, and I was invited here to help Alotta crack the code, which means I would hardly steal the thing! But yes, I was in her corridor at the time you say. I waited until Telly and that poor girl Hilaria had left, and I did intend to sneak into Alotta's room. I'm not proud of it, but I was hoping to catch a glimpse of the scroll before everyone else saw it. When I saw the door to her room was open, though, I lost my nerve and returned to finish dinner with the others.

Sounds like an eventful dinner, but does this rule anyone out? They all have explanations as to why they were in the corridor, but nothing they have said holds up as evidence that they didn't steal the scroll. It's time to see whether Alotta's cabin holds any more clues.

During a thorough search of her living quarters, you find two items of interest. The first is a crumpled-up piece of paper; the second is a napkin.

You start by focusing on the piece of paper. It's quite puzzling. The highlighted squares must mean something.

 HARTIGAN'S HINT: The time log listing the movements in the corridor is fact. Beware that some of the suspects may be lying about the reasoning behind their comings and goings.

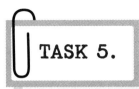

On closer inspection, you recognize that this is a puzzle to solve.

Each row, column, and 3 × 2 block must be filled out with the numbers 1–6 without repeating any numbers in the same row, column, or block. Do not guess; you must use process of elimination. For every number that you place, check along the row *and* along the column to make sure it has not been used before.

Read the numbers in the shaded boxes, from top to bottom, left to right and record them below.

What is the code?

Where have you seen these numbers before?

_____

Answer on page 188

1	3				
			5		
5	6			1	
2		4	3	5	6
6			1		4

HARTIGAN'S HINT:
Remember, in each 3 × 2
block, the numbers 1–6 can
only appear once.

1	2	3
4	5	6

That's right, it's the four-digit code for the safe. Someone must have stolen this information from Alotta and used it to open her safe.

You check the paper for fingerprints and find not one but *two* usable prints!

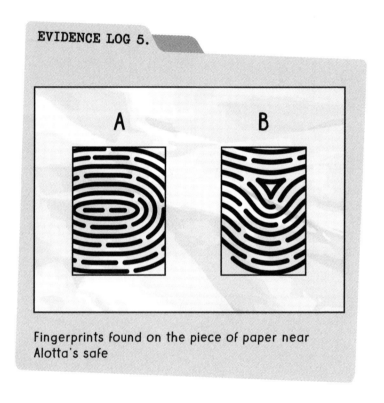

EVIDENCE LOG 5.

A   B

Fingerprints found on the piece of paper near Alotta's safe

TASK 6.

Can you work out who they belong to?

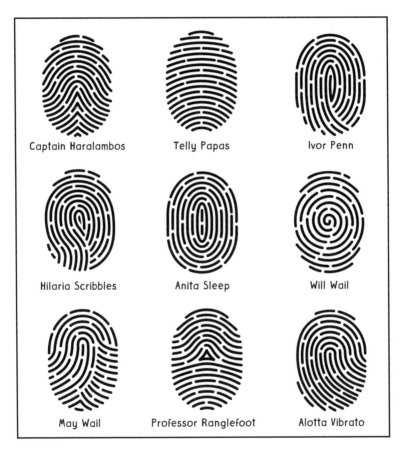

Captain Haralambos   Telly Papas   Ivor Penn

Hilaria Scribbles   Anita Sleep   Will Wail

May Wail   Professor Ranglefoot   Alotta Vibrato

Fingerprint **A** belongs to: _____

Fingerprint **B** belongs to: _____

Answer on page 189

You now turn your attention to the second item you uncovered in Alotta's cabin: the napkin. Perhaps it will offer up more clues as to who stole the scroll.

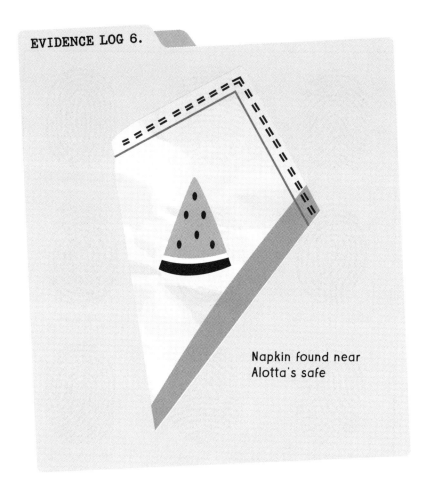

Napkin found near
Alotta's safe

Alotta confirms it is one of the napkins used at dinner the night before. Each guest had a different image embroidered on the front of their napkin.

Notes:

TASK 7.

Can you determine who had the watermelon napkin based on the information provided below?

- Hilaria rather hoped she wasn't sitting next to Alotta, but she was.

- Will complained that he had a flamingo looming over him all evening.

- Despite being hit by a tentacle projectile from Ivor Penn, who was sitting directly opposite her, Hilaria did not have the octopus napkin. It was either an ice cream or an ice pop.

- The side Will was sitting on meant the sea was to his left.

- Ivor Penn had a picture of fruit on his napkin.

- Telly was farthest away from Alotta and on an end seat so he could leave the table and serve with ease.

- There was one person between May and her husband, Will.

- Captain Haralambos had either a jellyfish or an octopus on his napkin.

- The side the captain was sitting on meant the sea was to his right.

- Anita either had a shell or a palm tree on her napkin.

38

Fill in the names in the boxes to determine who was sitting where and who had which napkin at dinner.

Anita Sleep   Professor Ranglefoot

May Wail   Ivor Penn

Captain Haralambos   Telly Papas

Hilaria Scribbles   Will Wail

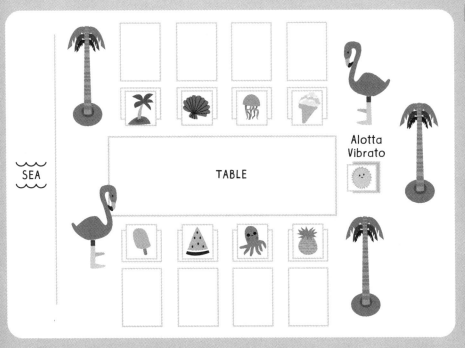

From your evidence, can you make an accusation?

Who is your prime suspect?

_____

Answer on page 189

You make your way to Professor Ranglefoot's cabin, ready to accuse him of stealing the scroll. When you get there, he is lying face down, unconscious on the floor! You note the time on his digital clock is 11:02 a.m., and when you roll him over, you see that his whole face is swollen and as red as a baboon's bottom. It appears that he may have had an allergic reaction to something.

Do you remember what the professor is allergic to?

You call for help. Captain Haralambos is there in a flash and administers an EpiPen.

Thankfully, the professor comes around. His eyes flash to the bedside table. You ask him whether something is wrong.

"The scroll is gone!" he wails.

So, you were correct, he *did* steal it!

But now someone has stolen it from *him*. It's time to move on to **Case 2: The Professor's Poisoner!**

Answer on page 189

Take note of the key pieces of evidence
and people involved so far:

CASE 2:
THE PROFESSOR'S POISONER

Professor Ranglefoot is taken to the sickbay to be looked after by Telly Papas. You set out to update Alotta Vibrato on the case and find her on the top deck relaying details of her life as Hilaria Scribbles takes notes.

When Alotta sees you, she dismisses Hilaria. Looking rather relieved, Hilaria collects her things. As she passes you, a piece of paper slips from her notebook onto the floor. You pick it up, immediately recognizing that it has been written in code. You try to memorize the letters, but she snatches it from you, saying, "Just my shorthand notes."

Alotta inquires whether you have found the culprit and you tell her that Professor Ranglefoot was the person who stole the scroll from the safe. She asks you how he got the code.

Who do you believe gave the code to the professor?

With all the bluster she can muster, Alotta bellows for Anita. When Anita appears, Alotta asks why her fingerprints were on a note containing information about the code to her safe. Clearly flustered, Anita says the professor told her he only wanted to look at it and offered to pay €100 for the code. Anita said she only did it because she needed the money. Alotta informs her that she will be needing a new job now, too.

"I shall have both Professor Ranglefoot and Anita sent back to the mainland to be dealt with by the police!" Alotta says, but you convince her that they should stay until the scroll has been found. You may need to question them further, and they're not going anywhere as long as they're on the boat.

Alotta clutches her hand to her chest. "What do you mean until it's been found? You just told me Professor Ranglefoot took it!"

You break the news that he was poisoned, probably with eggs, and the scroll has been stolen . . . again.

 HARTIGAN'S HINT: Who is closest to Alotta and left their fingerprints on the note?

Answer on page 190

"Oh, for goodness' sake!" she cries. "Who stole it this time?"

You tell her you don't know, but you're determined to find out.

It's time to head back to the sickbay to ask the professor more questions, but you can't get that slip of paper that Hilaria dropped out of your head. You only held it for a moment, but you do remember some of the letters. It looked like a simple alphabet reversal cipher to you. It may not be important to your case, but you know not to dismiss anything. Everyone is a suspect. You quickly jot down everything you remember.

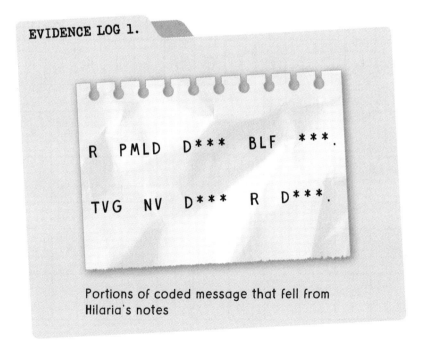

EVIDENCE LOG 1.

R PMLD D*** BLF ***.

TVG NV D*** R D***.

Portions of coded message that fell from Hilaria's notes

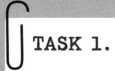

TASK 1.

Are your instincts correct? Is this a simple alphabet reversal cipher? To check, look at the top row where the alphabet is backward, search for the first code letter, and write the letter underneath it in the answer grid.

Z	Y	X	W	V	U	T	S	R	Q	P	O	N
A	B	C	D	E	F	G	H	I	J	K	L	M

R

P	M	L	D

D	*	*	*

T	V	G

N	V

D	*	*	*

 HARTIGAN'S HINT: Once you have translated all the letters available, can you use your powers of deduction to work out any of the missing letters represented by the asterisks?

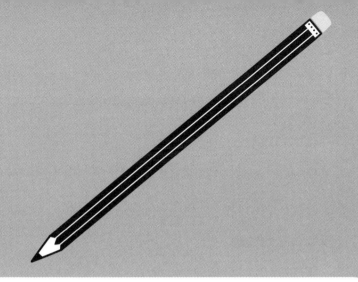

M	L	K	J	I	H	G	F	E	D	C	B	A
N	O	P	Q	R	S	T	U	V	W	X	Y	Z

B	L	F

*	*	*

.

R

D	*	*	*

.

Answer on page 190

It does seem like an alphabet reversal cipher, but it is difficult to make out what the message is saying with so many letters missing.

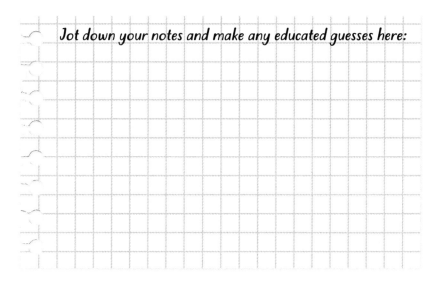

Jot down your notes and make any educated guesses here:

Maybe the meaning will become clear later in your investigation.

You continue on your way to see Professor Ranglefoot in the sickbay to find out whether he remembers seeing anything that might help you discover who poisoned him and made off with the scroll.

Much of the swelling has gone down, but his lips and eyes are still quite puffy. He immediately apologizes for lying to you about taking the scroll.

"I was so overcome with desire that I acted in a manner quite out of character." He lowers his voice. "You see, searching for that lost music has been my obsession for most of my adult life—ever since I discovered that there was a code buried within the musical notes that will lead to something incredible."

A code hidden in the notes? That *is* interesting! You ask what "incredible something" he's talking about, and he pulls a pair of photographs from his pocket.

"I have my theories, and these should confirm them."

You take the first photograph from him. You see what it is, but you have no idea what it means, and you look at him, confused.

Pegasus statue

"My research into the lost music led me to the Pegasus statue in Corinth, in Greece," the professor explains. "And this . . ." he continues.

"This is a photograph of the bottom of the statue's raised hoof,"
he finishes.

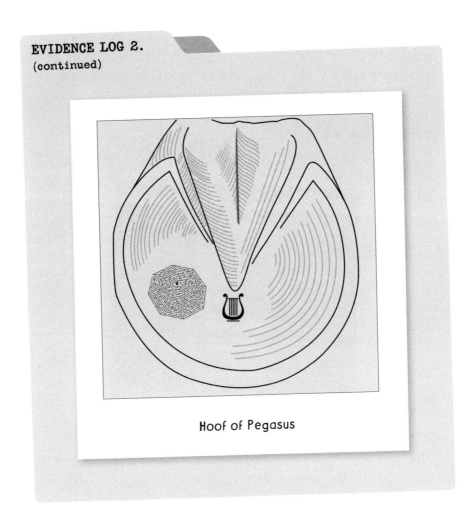

Hoof of Pegasus

On closer inspection, you spot two small images not so well hidden within the photograph of the hoof. You use your trusty magnifying glass to get a better look.

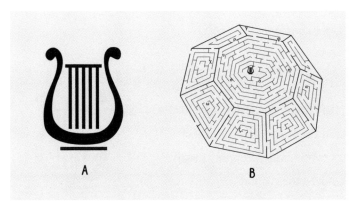

Image A is a lyre, an instrument popular in ancient Greece, and a symbol for music.

Image B appears to be a maze of sorts.

Professor Ranglefoot sees you squinting at the photograph with your magnifying glass.

"Yes, they are incredibly small and, for that reason, have gone unnoticed for years. I believe that, once solved, this puzzle will confirm the existence of an artifact of unbelievable importance linked to the missing notes of *The Pegasus* opera. I had the image of the maze professionally enlarged and discovered there are letters hidden within it, but despite my best efforts, I have failed to figure out what it means."

Professor Ranglefoot may have come up short, but I'm sure someone with your intellect will be able to solve it.

You ask him if you can give it a try.

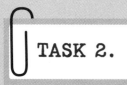

TASK 2.

Solve the maze to discover what Professor Ranglefoot hopes the code may lead to.

First, find your way to the lyre at the center of the maze. If you take the correct route, you will pass through six Greek letters. Write them down.

a lyre

α	β	γ	δ	ε	ζ
Alpha	Beta	Gamma	Delta	Epsilon	Zeta
η	θ	ι	κ	λ	μ
Eta	Theta	Iota	Kappa	Lambda	Mu
ν	ζ	ο	π	ρ	σ/ς
Nu	Xi	Omicron	Pi	Rho	Sigma
τ	υ	φ	χ	ψ	ω
Tau	Upsilon	Phi	Chi	Pai	Omega

 HARTIGAN'S HINT: The ancient Greek alphabet by itself has no accents, but some letters take accents in order to make certain words.

ENTER

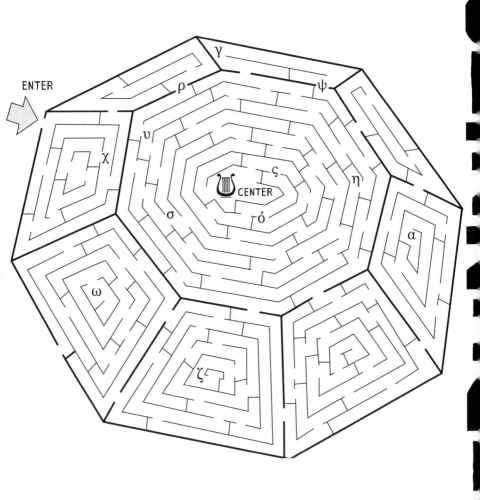

Write the six Greek letters: _ _ _ _ _ _

Answer on page 191

TASK 3.

Once you have reached the center of the maze, you need to find your way to the exit. If you choose the correct path, you will pass through four more Greek letters. Write these down, too.

α Alpha	β Beta	γ Gamma	δ Delta	ε Epsilon	ζ Zeta
η Eta	θ Theta	ι Iota	κ Kappa	λ Lambda	μ Mu
ν Nu	ζ Xi	ο Omicron	π Pi	ρ Rho	σ/ς Sigma
τ Tau	υ Upsilon	φ Phi	χ Chi	ψ Pai	ω Omega

 HARTIGAN'S HINT: The ancient Greek alphabet by itself has no accents, but some letters take accents in order to make certain words.

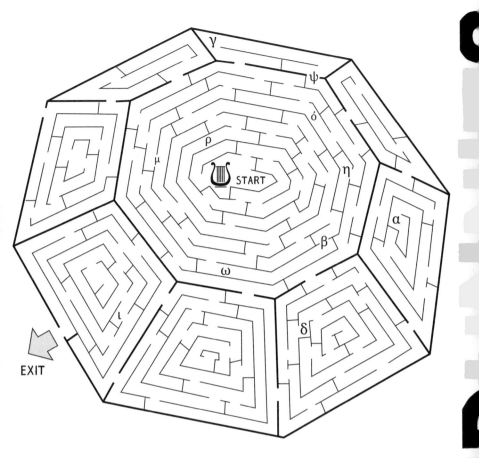

EXIT

Write the four Greek letters: _ _ _ _

Superb work! From these two sets of letters, you have found two Greek words. Now it's time to figure out what they mean and discover what the code in the missing music leads to!

 HARTIGAN'S HINT: Sometimes starting
at the exit can give you fresh perspective.

Answer on page 191

Translate the Greek for the first set of letters you collected when you headed *into* the maze.

α Alpha	β Beta	γ Gamma	δ Delta	ε Epsilon	ζ Zeta
η Eta	θ Theta	ι Iota	κ Kappa	λ Lambda	μ Mu
ν Nu	ζ Xi	ο Omicron	π Pi	ρ Rho	σ/ς Sigma
τ Tau	υ Upsilon	φ Phi	χ Chi	ψ Pai	ω Omega

Professor Ranglefoot seems to think that the first set of letters will spell out a material. Which one could it be? Use the clues below to help you translate.

- *Marble* starts with **Mu**.
- *Gold* includes the letter **Rho**.
- *Bronze* includes the letter **Pi**.
- Both *silver* and *marble* include the letter **Alpha**.

Draw lines to match the English word to its correct ancient Greek counterpart in the box below.

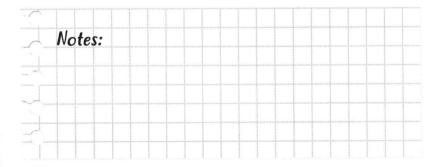

SILVER	μάρμαρο
BRONZE	χρυσός
MARBLE	ασήμι
GOLD	μπρούντζος

Notes:

What is the first word you discovered in the maze?

Answer on page 192

TASK 5.

Professor Ranglefoot believes that the second word, **ρόδι**, may be a type of fruit. Use the translating machine to determine which one.

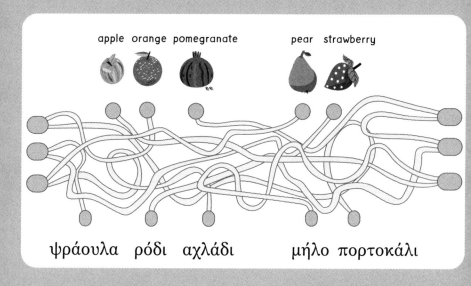

apple   orange   pomegranate   pear   strawberry

ψράουλα   ρόδι   αχλάδι   μήλο   πορτοκάλι

Your answer is _____.

 HARTIGAN'S HINT: There's a big clue on the cover of this book!

Answer on page 192

58

Notes:

The maze on the bottom of the Pegasus statue suggests the code in the missing music will lead to a *gold pomegranate*—how very extraordinary! There is more to this case than you realized. You ask the professor what the gold pomegranate is.

Professor Ranglefoot spreads his arms wide, his still-puffy eyes shining. "It is a pomegranate made of gold."

You quickly realize you need to be clearer in your questioning and ask him what is so special about it.

"The Golden Pomegranate is the unknown eighth Wonder of the World!"

You tell him you understood there to be only seven wonders.

"That is why I said *unknown*—very few people are aware of the Golden Pomegranate. The pomegranate features heavily in Greek mythology; it was the only thing Persephone could eat when Hades kidnapped her and kept her in the underworld. It is said that the Golden Pomegranate will bring its owner love, beauty, marriage, fertility, rebirth, hope, prosperity, and . . . eternal life!"

You tell him that all you had heard was that pomegranates were a good source of vitamin C. Surely, those other claims are nonsense—or at the very least, overreaching?

"Perhaps," he agrees, "but the Golden Pomegranate is also worth an enormous amount of money."

Which, you suppose, is why someone wanted to poison him to get the scroll. You jot down in your notes: *The scroll leads to the missing music, which will lead to the Golden Pomegranate.* Your case just got a *lot* more interesting!

You turn your attention back to the poisoning and ask the professor if he has any idea who might be responsible. Unfortunately, he doesn't. He does have an idea how they did it, though. He believes the milkshake he drank was laced with egg.

"I had taken it down to my room to drink away from the glaring sun, and I immediately began feeling quite unwell. When I looked for my EpiPen, it was not in the drawer where I put it. As I passed out, I sensed someone entering my room. While I did not see them, I remember it was exactly 11:01 a.m., as I saw the digital clock change before the black descended."

After a swift investigation, you determine where everybody was on the *Icarus Infinity* at 11:00 a.m. Whoever attacked Professor Ranglefoot only had one minute to get to his cabin. If you can work out how long it would take each person to reach Professor Ranglefoot, you should be able to rule out anyone who would take longer than a minute to get to him. You time the distances from each passenger's location to the professor's cabin.

Use the ship's plans on page 64 to see where each suspect was located at 11:00 a.m. Apply the information below to help you figure out how long it would take each person to get to Professor Ranglefoot's cabin on the bottom deck.

- Every set of stairs takes 15 seconds to descend.

- The time it takes to get from the stairs near the stern of the ship to the stairs in the middle is 10 seconds.

- There is only *one* set of stairs that leads down from the owner's deck to the bottom deck.

- On the bottom deck, the time it takes to get from the stairs to Professor Ranglefoot's cabin is 20 seconds.

- On the top deck, the time it takes to get from the captain's bridge to the closest stairs is 25 seconds.

- Will and Ivor, who were sunbathing on the top deck, are 5 seconds from their closest staircase.

- Telly, Anita, and Hilaria were all right next to staircases, so their time reaching those staircases is 0 seconds.

- May did not descend any stairs.

- From her starting position, it would take May 15 seconds to get to the stairs on the bottom deck.

Suspect	Calculations	Time in seconds
CAPT. H.		
IVOR and WILL		
TELLY		
HILARIA		
ANITA		
MAY		

 HARTIGAN'S HINT: You can eliminate the suspects who would need longer than 60 seconds to get to Professor Ranglefoot's cabin.

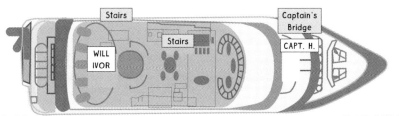

STERN

TOP DECK

STERN

MAIN DECK

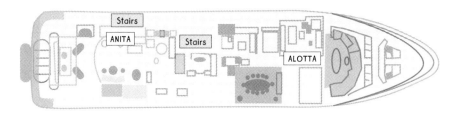

STERN

OWNER'S DECK

STERN

BOTTOM DECK

All that hard work was worth it! You have managed to eliminate three suspects.

Which four passengers are still in the picture?

_____

_____

_____

_____

That was some stupendously good calculating, my dear detective! Bravo! Having narrowed it down, you decide to focus on the suspected source of the poisoning: the milkshake. You speak to Alotta Vibrato and she confirms that she gave express instructions that there should be no eggs aboard the *Icarus Infinity*. She was well aware of Professor Ranglefoot's allergy and made sure everyone else knew about it, too. This means that whoever laced the milkshake must have stowed the eggs away in their luggage in order to sneak them onto the *Icaraus Infinity*. Alotta Vibrato insisted that all the luggage be scanned for security reasons before being allowed on the ship, so she can provide you with the images from those scans.

Answer on page 193

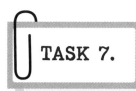

First, though, you will need to work out which suitcases your suspects own.

To solve this grid, place an ✗ where a statement isn't true and a ✔ if it is correct. The first one has been done for you.

		Color				Logo			
		RED	BROWN	WHITE	GRAY	TRIANGLE	SQUARE	DIAMOND	CIRCLE
Suspects	ANITA			✗					
	MAY								
	HILARIA								
	TELLY								
Logo	TRIANGLE								
	SQUARE								
	DIAMOND								
	CIRCLE								

 HARTIGAN'S HINT: If you place a check mark, what can you now cross out?

- Anita would not choose an impractical color like white for a suitcase.

- The logo on Telly's suitcase does not have four sides.

- Hilaria would not choose a suitcase in brown or gray as they are hard to spot on the luggage carousel.

- The suitcase with a triangle logo is not gray or white.

- The diamond is either on the red or white suitcase.

- Neither May nor Telly has a brown suitcase.

- If Anita has a brown suitcase, the logo on the white suitcase is a diamond.

- Either Anita or Telly has a gray suitcase.

- The person whose suitcase has the square logo has five letters in their first name.

- If the white suitcase has a diamond logo it belongs to May.

Name	Suitcase description
ANITA	
MAY	
HILARIA	
TELLY	

Answer on page 194

TASK 8.

It's time to take a look at whose suitcase contained the eggs. A computer software malfunction has caused the scanned images of the suitcases to become scrambled—pun absolutely intended! Can you spot the eggs in one of the suitcases?

EGGS

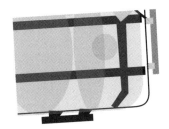

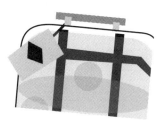

 HARTIGAN'S HINT:
Look closely at the
suitcase logos.

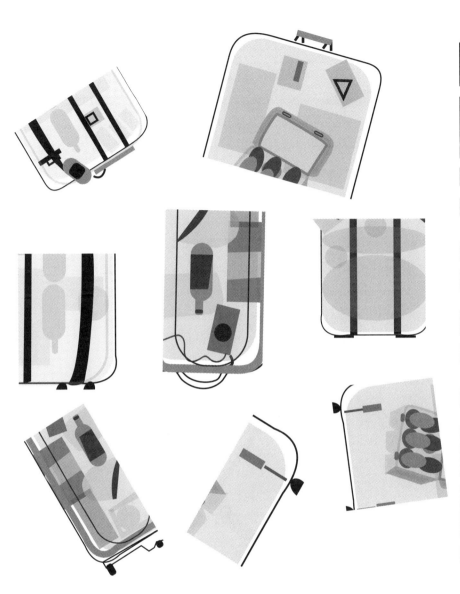

Which suitcase contained the eggs?

_____

Who does it belong to? _____

Answer on page 195

You arrive at Hilaria Scribbles's room and, when faced with your egg-based evidence, she admits to poisoning the professor. Apparently, she brought the eggs aboard the *Icarus Infinity* as part of her high-protein diet. Very infuriatingly, she also says that she no longer has the scroll.

She tells you that she was blackmailed into stealing the scroll and has already left it somewhere for the blackmailer to collect. You are skeptical of this supposed blackmailing—perhaps she still has the scroll stashed somewhere for safekeeping—but she holds up the piece of paper with the coded message that you partially deciphered earlier as proof. Hilaria reveals that this is the message the blackmailer sent to her.

Finish deciphering the code to discover whether Hilaria
is telling the truth.

R PMLD DSZG BLF WRW.

_ ____ ____ ___ ___.

TVG NV DSZG R DZMG.

___ __ ____ _ ____.

Alphabet reversal cipher:

Z	Y	X	W	V	U	T	S	R	Q	P	O	N	M	L	K	J	I	H	G	F	E	D	C	B	A
A	B	C	D	E	F	G	H	I	J	K	L	M	N	O	P	Q	R	S	T	U	V	W	X	Y	Z

Answer on page 195

It would appear someone *is* blackmailing her! However, their use of the simple alphabet reversal code implies that you're not dealing with a criminal mastermind.

Hilaria shows you another note, this one giving her instructions to leave the scroll in a bag inside the toilet tank on the main deck. When you check the tank, it is no longer there. Whoever blackmailed Hilaria has already made off with the scroll.

You have now solved two cases of theft and one case of poisoning. You already have much to report to the police on your return to port, but you aren't finished yet! You still don't have the scroll, and now you have a blackmailer to catch. It's time to move on to **Case 3: The Toilet Tank Blackmailer.**

Review the key pieces of evidence
and people involved so far:

CASE 3:

THE TOILET TANK BLACKMAILER

Despite your ferocious questioning, Hilaria insists she doesn't know who blackmailed her. All she says is that they know something about her that would be extremely damaging to her professionally if it gets out, hence why she was willing to do anything to stop that from happening.

It's time to find out a little more about Hilaria Scribbles and see whether you can discover what she is trying to hide. And because she mentioned the information would harm her professionally, you start by looking into her work.

Your research shows she has received many glowing reviews for her writing, but one negative review in particular catches your eye.

TREVELYN MONTAGUE-SMYTHE

★★★★★ *A masterpiece!*

Reviewed on February 1

One rarely finds a book that transcends the boundaries of thought, but such is the case with *My Feet Have Toes*. This is not merely a collection of philosophical musings—it is a masterpiece that unfolds the layers of existence. Bravo, Ms. Scribbles!

BRIAN TUBEROUS

★★★★★ *As irresistible as potato chips*

Reviewed on July 17
Verified Purchase

I thought this was going to be a book about potatoes. I like potatoes. But this book wasn't really about potatoes. I'm not exactly sure what it was about to be honest. But the paper smelled nice, so I give it 5 stars!

OPUS MEGALOS

★☆☆☆☆ *Hilaria Scribbles will get her comeuppance!*

Reviewed on November 12
Verified Purchase

This review has been removed as it goes against website policy.

PETER PUMPLEDINK

★★★★★ *Already a classic*

Reviewed on July 17
Verified Purchase

The Potato moved me to tears and changed not only how I view potatoes, but how I view myself. I shall try to be more potato from now on!

It sounds like Opus has an issue with Hilaria, but there's no Megalos aboard the *Icarus Infinity*.

You also find a review in *The Daily Wail* written by none other than Ivor Penn!

Hilaria Scribbles's second book, *My Feet Have Toes*, has been widely praised and is expected to win all the major book prizes. I appear to be the only one who did not enjoy it. On opening the first page, Scribbles transported me to a dimension where time moves slower than a sloth in molasses. There is nothing new in what she has written; in fact, I have a strong feeling that I have read something like this before.

★☆☆☆☆

- IVOR PENN FOR *THE DAILY WAIL*

It's clear that Ivor is not a fan of Hilaria's writing, but that doesn't necessarily mean he is the one blackmailing her. That said, the connection between them cannot be ignored, so you head to his cabin to conduct a search for any incriminating evidence that may link him to the blackmail.

Inside, you find a locked briefcase. You conduct a quick scan of the room and notice a large bunch of keys on the bedside table.

TASK 1.

Determine which key is the one that will open the
briefcase. Circle your answer.

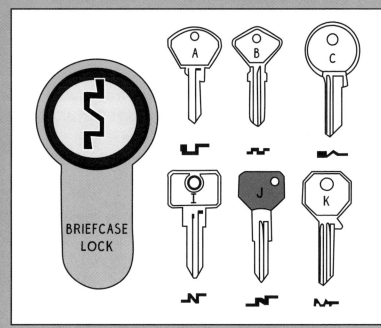

BRIEFCASE
LOCK

Answer on page 196

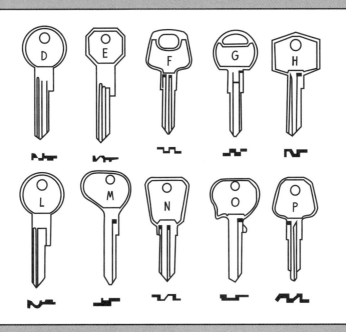

Superb work! Inside the briefcase is a laptop. It is password protected, but there is a sticky note attached to the screen that must be a clue to what the password is.

| FY | GX | HW | _ _ |
| FX | IV | LT | _ _ |

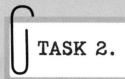

TASK 2.

To unlock the laptop, you have to enter a four-letter password. You can crack the password using the sequence of numbers from the sticky note. The arrows below point to the first pair of letters in each sequence. Can you work out what comes next in both patterns?

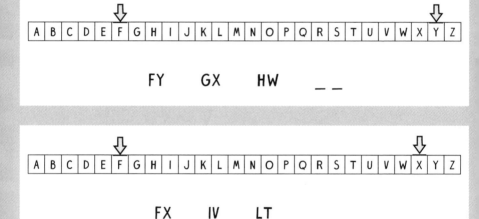

| A | B | C | D | E | F | G | H | I | J | K | L | M | N | O | P | Q | R | S | T | U | V | W | X | Y | Z |

FY   GX   HW   _ _

| A | B | C | D | E | F | G | H | I | J | K | L | M | N | O | P | Q | R | S | T | U | V | W | X | Y | Z |

FX   IV   LT   _ _

Combine the two missing letters from the first sequence with the two missing letters from the last sequence. What is the password?

HARTIGAN'S HINT: Draw arrows for the next pairs of letters in the clue. What happens to the first letter in each pair and what happens to the second letter? Can you see a pattern?

Answers on page 197

How extraordinary! Ivor Penn employed quite a complicated reminder for such an easy password. People never cease to amaze!

You open up his documents and spot a folder labeled "HS." If this is about Hilaria Scribbles, it does not look good for Ivor.

HS

You open the folder and click on a document titled "OM."

OM

EVIDENCE LOG 2.

National Library of Greece records:

a) ⋈ ⊓ ΔΓ|||

b) ✕✕✕HHⵎΔΔ||

The document lists two numbers, written in the old Greek number system, that appear to relate to two records held at the National Library of Greece.

TASK 3.

If you can work out what these two numbers are, you should be able to look them up in the library's records. And hopefully, once you've accessed the records, they will give you more information related to what Ivor Penn has on Hilaria.

I	II	III	IIII	Γ	ΓI	ΓII	ΓIII	ΓIIII	△
1	2	3	4	5	6	7	8	9	10

△Γ	△△	⟨△⟩	H	⟨Γ⟩	X	⟨X⟩	M	⟨M⟩	)
15	20	50	100	500	1,000	5,000	10,000	50,000	¼

a)
⟨X⟩ =

⟨Γ⟩ =

△ =

Γ =

III =

Total = _____

 HARTIGAN'S HINT: First identify what number each symbol represents, then add them up.

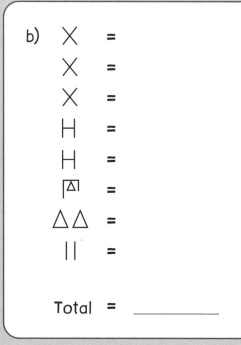

b)
X =
X =
X =
H =
H =
⊓⊿ =
△△ =
|| =

Total = _____

Interestingly, the library's records for those numbers lead you to two books, written by ... wait for it ... Opus Megalos! Could it be the same Opus Megalos who left Hilaria a one-star review? The first book is titled Η πατάτα, which translates to *The Potato*, and the second book title translates to *There Are Toes on My Feet*! They were both published in the 1990s—a long time before Hilaria wrote her books. It looks like Hilaria stole someone else's work and passed it off as her own—and it seems that Ivor Penn *knew* Hilaria was a plagiarist and used the information to blackmail her into stealing the scroll!

You conduct a thorough search of Ivor's room to see if he has stashed the scroll nearby. It is nowhere to be found, but you *do* discover a book on his bedside table that may be of interest.

Answer on page 198

GREEK GODS
SHOW THE WAY

A SECRET AND
VERY RARE BOOK

The "secret and very rare book"
on Ivor's bedside table

There's a lyre on the cover—the Greek symbol for music!
And next to it is a drawing of what looks like a pomegranate
covered with unusual black spots. Based on context clues, this
book must have something to do with the lost music and the
Golden Pomegranate. Ivor Penn is clearly undertaking his own
investigation. Which means that, right now, he is your top suspect
for being in possession of Alotta's scroll.

You make a copy of the pomegranate on the front cover for evidence in case you need it later.

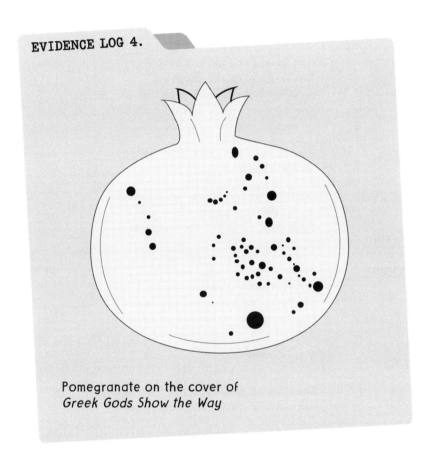

EVIDENCE LOG 4.

Pomegranate on the cover of
Greek Gods Show the Way

You turn your attention back to the book and flip through, stopping at a page that has been furiously highlighted.

Name	Role	Power Level
APHRODITE	Goddess of beauty and love. Daughter of Zeus and Hera.	75
APOLLO	God of music, arts, knowledge, healing, plague, prophecy, poetry, beauty, and archery. Son of Zeus. Twin brother of Artemis.	86
ARES	God of courage, war, bloodshed, and violence.	83
ARTEMIS	Goddess of the hunt, wilderness, animals, the moon, and youth. Daughter of Zeus. Twin sister of Apollo.	80
ATHENA	Goddess of reason, wisdom, intelligence, skill, peace, warfare, battle strategy, and handicrafts. Daughter of Zeus.	89
DEIMOS (TERROR)	Son of Ares.	38
DEMETER	Goddess of grain, agriculture, harvest, growth, and nourishment.	68
DIONYSUS	God of wine, fruitfulness, parties, festivals, madness, drunkenness, vegetation, ecstasy, and the theater.	54
ERIS (STRIFE)	Goddess of war. Sister of Ares.	37
FURIES	Goddesses of revenge.	63

Name	Role	Power Level
HADES	God of the underworld, the dead, and wealth. Brother of Zeus.	92
HERA	Queen of the gods. Goddess of the sky, women, marriage, childbirth, heirs, kings, and empires. Wife and sister of Zeus.	90
HERMES	God of boundaries, travel, trade, communication, language, writing, cunning, and thieves. Son of Zeus.	90
HYPERION	God of light.	64
HYPNOS	God of sleep. Brother of Thanatos.	44
IRIS	Divine messenger of the gods.	12
MUSES	Goddesses of music. Daughters of Zeus.	14
PERSEPHONE	Queen of the underworld. Goddess of spring. Wife of Hades. Partial to pomegranates.	45
POSEIDON	Major Olympian god. The Earthshaker. God of the sea, rivers, floods, droughts, and earthquakes. Brother of Zeus.	95
THANATOS (DEATH)	Escorts souls to the afterlife.	48
ZEUS	Most powerful of all gods. Cloud gatherer. Lord of the lightning bolt. Son of Cronos.	100

Unsure what any of it means, you are forward-thinking enough to know that it could prove important. For a moment, you consider tearing out the page, but thankfully you decide against committing such a heinous act of vandalism* and instead choose to take the book with you to borrow until the case is solved.

Between the files Ivor has collected on Hilaria, and his obvious interest in the Golden Pomegranate, you have sufficient evidence to accuse him of having blackmailed Hilaria for the scroll. This means it is time for a confrontation. Ooh, I do love this bit!

However, confronting someone means finding them, and locating Mr. Penn has proved rather challenging. You search the *Icarus Infinity*, but he is nowhere to be seen. Drat and blast! The man appears to have vanished! Of course, this is impossible; he *has* to be somewhere on this ship, and wherever he is, you shall find him in **Case 4: Why Can You Never Find a Penn When You Need One?**

As you may recall from The Case of the Dumpleton Diamond, *I am not in the habit of destroying books.*

Discoveries so far:

CASE 4:

WHY CAN YOU NEVER FIND A PENN WHEN YOU NEED ONE?

C aptain Haralambos says that if someone isn't on a boat, the only other place they could be is in the ocean. Gosh, let's hope that isn't the case! It will be difficult to complete the investigation if Ivor Penn is at the bottom of the sea. You confirm with the captain that Ivor hasn't escaped on the speedboat that the *Icarus Infinity* tows along (the same one that ferried you from the dock to the yacht). Maybe Ivor *has* fallen overboard! The captain puts out a call to other ships to see whether anyone has seen a journalist bobbing about in the Aegean Sea. He then declares that he and Telly will search the *Icarus Infinity* one more time to see if they have any luck finding Ivor or a clue to his whereabouts.

As they are leaving the captain's bridge, you notice a red flashing light on the ship's radar system and ask Captain Haralambos what it is. He tells you that it is there just to let him know that there is another ship nearby. He heads off to search for Ivor, but you sense he is not being honest with you. The ship's navigation system shows nearby vessels as diamonds. The flashing light is circular.

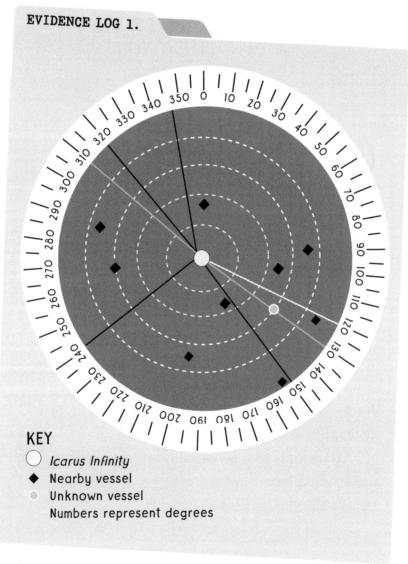

EVIDENCE LOG 1.

KEY
○ *Icarus Infinity*
◆ Nearby vessel
○ Unknown vessel
Numbers represent degrees

You look at the rest of the control board . . .

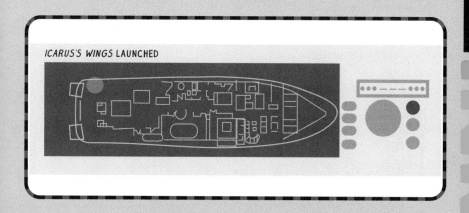

. . . and see that *Icarus's Wings*, the *Infinity*'s life raft, has been launched! Did Ivor Penn use it to escape? It's hard to believe he'd be foolish enough to paddle a life raft across the Mediterranean, but his password *was* his own name, so who knows? Isn't it also suspicious that Captain Haralambos neglected to tell you that the life raft had been deployed? Someone with his sailing experience would have noticed the warning signal.

On the control board, next to a red light, there's a volume dial. When you turn it, a tapping noise plays through a speaker. Dots and dashes. It's Morse code!

TASK 1.

Use the key below to decipher the message as it comes through the speaker.

A	• —	J	• — — —	S	• • •
B	— • • •	K	— • —	T	—
C	— • — •	L	• — • •	U	• • —
D	— • •	M	— —	V	• • • —
E	•	N	— •	W	• — —
F	• • — •	O	— — —	X	— • • —
G	— — •	P	• — — •	Y	— • — —
H	• • • •	Q	— — • —	Z	— — • •
I	• •	R	• — •		

 HARTIGAN'S HINT: Each set of dots and dashes represents one letter.

• • • •   •   • _ • •   • _ _ •

___ ___   ___ ___   ___ ___   ___ ___

• _ • •   _ _ _   • • •   _

___ ___   ___ ___   ___ ___   ___ ___

• _   _

___ ___   ___ ___

• • •   •   • _

___ ___   ___ ___   ___ ___

• •   • • • _   _ _ _   • _ •

___ ___   ___ ___   ___ ___   ___ ___

Answer on page 199

It's Ivor Penn calling for help from *Icarus's Wings*. Oh, this is good news—the prime suspect hasn't drowned! You radio the coast guard; they ask for his location and confirm that they'll collect him.

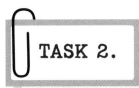

TASK 2.

Look back to Evidence Log 1 on page 92 to determine the bearings where the coast guard will find Ivor Penn bobbing about in a life raft.

_____ **degrees**

After the coast guard has picked him up, they send you a message that may explain how Ivor found himself so far from land in an inflatable dinghy.

EVIDENCE LOG 2.

Mr. Penn does not know how he came to be floating about in the middle of the sea. He remembers leaving his room to get some ice cream—the next moment, he came around in a life raft with a thumping headache. It appears that he may have suffered a blow to the head from a blunt instrument. He has no idea why anyone would do this, nor who it was.

 HARTIGAN'S HINT: The symbol for the unknown vessel is in line with which number of degrees?   *Answer on page 199*

It sounds like Ivor was attacked. While he claims not to know why, he is probably being tight-lipped because he knows he can't acknowledge the stolen scroll. The coast guard did not mention it in the list of items Ivor had with him. It appears there is yet another thief aboard the *Icarus Infinity*! One might say that Alotta Vibrato's guests are rather more suited to a pirate ship than a superyacht.

So now you must discover who walloped Ivor over the head and cast him off on *Icarus's Wings*. It could be Hilaria—Ivor was blackmailing her after all—though it would not be a very smart move on her part. She knew you were investigating who was responsible for stealing the scroll. Professor Ranglefoot has a deep interest in the Golden Pomegranate. He is still recovering in the sickbay, but he may have been capable. And then there's Captain Haralambos, who purposely ignored the distress signal transmitted from *Icarus's Wings*.

Ivor Penn must have been attacked *after* he took the scroll from the toilet tank. Hilaria tells you she put it there at 1:15 p.m. It is now 5:30 p.m.

You know the direction and speed the *Icarus Infinity* has been traveling—so you should be able to work out roughly when Ivor was tipped out into the water, which would narrow down the time of the attack.

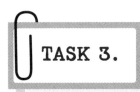

TASK 3.

You need to figure out what time Ivor went into the water. To do this, you must first determine how many knots, or nautical miles, the *Icarus Infinity* has sailed away from Ivor Penn in the "unknown vessel" (the small circular dot). Look at the distance each radar line represents.

EACH CONCENTRIC RADAR LINE = 15 KNOTS OR 15 NAUTICAL MILES

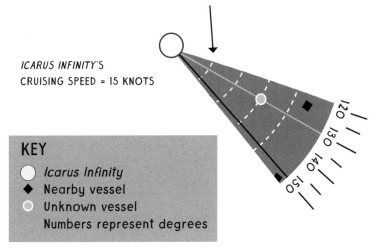

ICARUS INFINITY'S
CRUISING SPEED = 15 KNOTS

KEY
- ⬤ *Icarus Infinity*
- ◆ Nearby vessel
- ◎ Unknown vessel
- Numbers represent degrees

The *Icarus Infinity* has traveled _____ knots.

HARTIGAN'S HINT: To calculate the distance traveled, count each radar line and add up the total.

To determine the time taken, you must calculate how many hours it took to complete the distance traveled. The *Icarus Infinity* was traveling at 15 knots, or 15 nautical miles, an hour.

Divide the distance traveled by the speed at which the *Icarus* was traveling. This will give you the time in hours since Ivor went into the sea.

_____ ÷ _____ = _____
　　distance　　　　　　speed　　　　　　　time taken

Finally, in order to determine the time Ivor went into the water, you need to subtract the time taken since Ivor went into the sea from the time now.

5:30　　　　－ _____ = _____
time now　　　　time taken　　　time Ivor went into the water

Oh, I say, you really are a math whiz! Now that you have calculated the time of day Ivor went for an unexpected dip, you can find out who may have been responsible for pushing him in.

Answer on page 200

Alotta was with Anita and Hilaria from 2:00 to 4:00 p.m., giving them both a dressing-down for their behavior.

Will Wail had lunch with his wife, May, and when she went to see the professor, Will decided to have an afternoon siesta— apparently, he loves a good nap. Who doesn't?

Professor Ranglefoot had lunch in his cabin and then was joined by May Wail. They played cards from 1:35 to 3:00 p.m. He says May spent a lot of time asking him what he knew about the scroll.

Captain Haralambos says he was alone on the bridge, steering the boat the whole afternoon.

Telly Papas was cleaning up the ship from the time he served lunch at 1:00 p.m. until, well, he's probably still at it, to be honest.

This would suggest there are three suspects who were on their own and, therefore, don't have an alibi for the time Ivor was attacked.

List the three suspects here:

_____

_____

_____

The medical report from the coast guard who checked over Ivor Penn strongly suggests that he was struck on the back of the head with a heavy instrument. You search the boat and find three possible objects: a bronze bust of Alotta, a fire extinguisher, and a monkey-shaped lamp.

Answer on page 200

Notes and deductions:

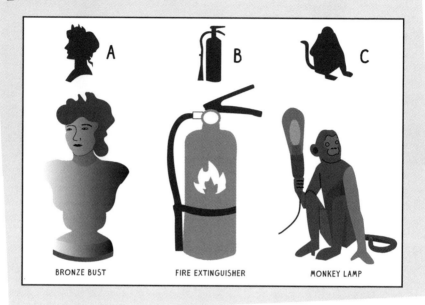

A

B

C

BRONZE BUST   FIRE EXTINGUISHER   MONKEY LAMP

- The monkey lamp was not found on the bottom deck.

- The fire extinguisher had this fingerprint (right) on the handle.

- Telly Papas was cleaning the bottom deck at the time Ivor disappeared. No one else was there.

- All the lamps on the main deck are in the shape of pineapples.

- Will Wail took a lamp from Alotta's cabin to his room on the owner's deck because his wasn't working.

- Fragments of bronze were found on the bottom deck.

 HARTIGAN'S HINT: You have seen this fingerprint before on page 35.

TASK 4.

First you will need to work out which suspect had which object and where they were on the ship. Place an ✗ where a statement isn't true and a ✔ if it is correct. The first one has been done for you.

		Suspect			Location		
		CAPTAIN HARALAMBOS	WILL WAIL	TELLY PAPAS	BOTTOM DECK	OWNER'S DECK	MAIN DECK
Object	(queen)						
	(fire extinguisher)						
	(monkey)				✗		
Location	BOTTOM DECK						
	OWNER'S DECK						
	MAIN DECK						

On your inspection of these three items, you notice that Alotta's bronze bust is without a nose. Alotta confirms that it definitely wasn't without a nose when she saw it that morning. The nose, you suspect, may have broken off in the attack on Ivor.

Who is now your prime suspect?

You head off to find him, ready to accuse him of attacking Ivor, sending him off to the blue beyond, and stealing the scroll, but you spot Telly doing something rather strange on the top deck and decide to hang back and observe. He is knotting rope around the yacht's railings.

Knotting ropes on a ship isn't unusual, but Telly is taking time to knot the ropes into intricate patterns. You wait until he leaves before you take a closer look. You realize you were correct to be curious. It's a coded message.

Since the dawn of time, people have found ingenious methods for communicating in secret. I once spent several weeks in South America learning all about quipu. Quipu was a method employed by the Incas and other ancient Andean cultures to keep records and communicate information using strings and knots. This does not look like an ancient Andean code, but it is definitely a code, and I have every confidence that you will figure it out.

Decipher the code knotted in the ropes.

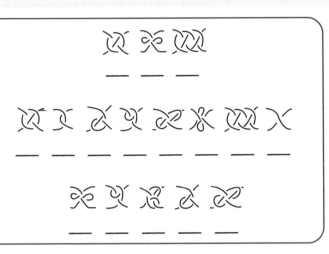

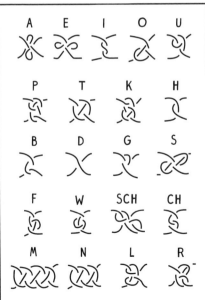

There's *knot* a lot that can outsmart you, is there? Top *knotch* work, detective!

Sorry. I'll stop now.

From what you have translated, it looks like Telly intends to sell the scroll to somebody aboard the *Icarus Infinity*, and he wants to keep the deal very secret indeed.

Your first instinct is that this is a message left for Captain Haralambos. Surely, his naval background makes him the person most likely to be able to read a message written in knots.

Perhaps a search of the captain's cabin is called for?

Inside Captain Haralambos's cabin, there are a laptop, four large maps on the wall, and numerous sailing charts, but your discerning gaze quickly settles on a locked safe, which looks just like the one in Alotta's cabin. You find a note taped on the back of it. It looks like it's another passcode reminder! It really is astonishing how many people are ignorant of the risks of leaving such valuable notes-to-self around. But it's good news for you!

Write yourself a reminder of the key pieces of evidence and people involved so far.

Who:

What:

Where:

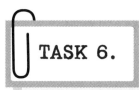

TASK 6.

Complete the number puzzle. One four-digit number will *not* fit into the grid. That, I predict, will be Captain Haralambos's code.

The first two numbers have been completed for you. 3649 should connect to a three-digit number that begins with a 4. Look at the list of three-digit numbers for one that begins with 4. Write it in the grid. This will give you the final digit of another three-digit number.

2 digits	3 digits	4 digits	5 digits	6 digits
25	342	1486	10453	403118
40	447	1538	54258	423567
58	~~614~~	2173	81941	
68	817	~~3649~~	83076	
	846	3621		
	985	6223		
		7812		
		9055		

 HARTIGAN'S HINT: Each number sequence will only fit once. Cross out each number once you've used it.

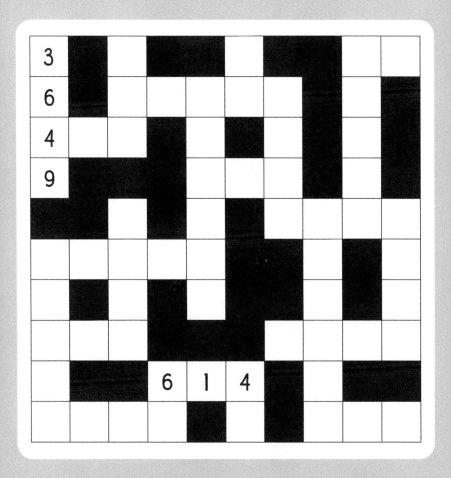

Captain Haralambos's passcode is: _____

Answer on page 202

Top job, my dear apprentice! Let's get that safe open!

You look inside and find a piece of rolled-up paper and gasp. Is it . . . ? Could it be . . . ? When you unroll the paper, you gasp again, this time in disappointment. This is not Alotta's stolen scroll. She described hers as having indecipherable shapes and lines on it. This scroll has no such thing. Instead, there is a drawing of a Pegasus, and quite an alarming-looking one at that.

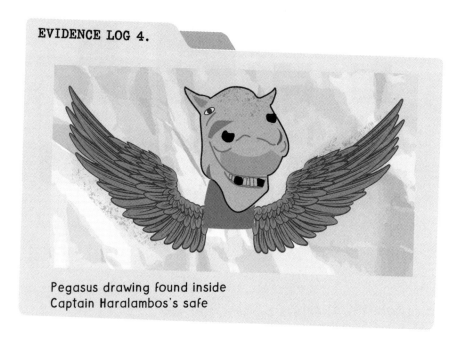

EVIDENCE LOG 4.

Pegasus drawing found inside
Captain Haralambos's safe

You notice that there are four holes in the paper. There's one in the eye region of the Pegasus, two in the mouth where teeth would be, and one where a nostril should be. The precise placement of the holes indicates they were made deliberately, rather than by wear and tear.

This is evidence that Captain Haralambos has an interest in the missing music of *The Pegasus*! You remember from the case notes you read on the plane that the captain had been a treasure hunter in the past—which means it's not a huge leap to believe that he knows the legend of the Golden Pomegranate and is hunting for that treasure, too.

While this is not conclusive proof that he is involved in the attack on Ivor, you copy the drawing down as best you can and take great care to get the holes in the exact right place.

I don't know quite what to say. This image is really rather disturbing. No matter! Evidence is evidence, whether it takes the form of an odd-looking Pegasus or not.

After you have completed your sketch, you notice there is a chart on the back of the paper.

Oh, I say! This is a find! It has the names of Greek gods on it and an image of a bespotted pomegranate that is identical to the one you found in Ivor Penn's cabin.

EVIDENCE LOG 5.

Point number	X	Y	
1	ZEUS − POSEIDON	HYPERION − FURIES	
2	HERA − ARES	ARES − ARTEMIS	
3	ARTEMIS ÷ (DEMETER − THANATOS)	(APOLLO − ARES) + (DEIMOS − ERIS)	
4	(DIONYSUS − THANATOS) + (PERSEPHONE − HYPNOS)	(DEMETER − DIONYSUS) ÷ MUSES	

Quickly, you get out the very secret and rare book, *Greek Gods Show the Way*. Let's hope they do. . . .

You theorize that the list of gods Ivor flagged in the book must be linked to the chart on the back of the Pegasus parchment! The columns labeled **X** and **Y** suggest this chart may be a clue to some coordinates. Could this clue finally lead to the missing music?

TASK 7.

Referencing the table on page 86, use the gods' power level stats to work out the values for **X** and **Y** below.

For example:

Point number	X
1	ZEUS − POSEIDON 100 - 95 = 5

This means that the **X** coordinate for the first point would be **5**.

Point number	X	Answers
1	ZEUS − POSEIDON	
2	HERA − ARES	
3	ARTEMIS ÷ (DEMETER − THANATOS)	
4	(DIONYSUS − THANATOS) + (PERSEPHONE − HYPNOS)	

 HARTIGAN'S HINT: When faced with multiple operations within the same equation, it's important that you perform the operations in the following order: parentheses, multiplication, division, addition, and then subtraction from left to right.

For example in the problem: (10 - 2) ÷ 4 =

You need to solve 10 - 2 in the parentheses first and then divide that answer by 4.

Once you complete the chart, you look at your findings. It is almost certain that you have decoded some coordinates, though with no map to plot them on, they aren't much use. There must be something you have found out that can help—but you draw a blank.

Fear not, I'm sure it will come to you. I always think it helps at moments like these to take some time to go over what you have learned so far. Perhaps something will jump out at you.

Y	Answers	Coordinates (X, Y)
HYPERION – FURIES		
ARES – ARTEMIS		
(APOLLO – ARES) + (DEIMOS – ERIS)		
(DEMETER – DIONYSUS) ÷ MUSES		

Answer on page 203

TASK 8.

Complete the crossword to review what you have already uncovered. Some of it may be useful, some of it not, but this investigation shows no signs of slowing, and you've got to keep your detective senses sharp!

Across

[2] Greek symbol for music
[3] What was drawn on the paper left in Alotta's safe?
[6] Winged animal in the title of the lost music
[8] The lost music may lead to the Golden _____
[10] Object with which Ivor was hit on the head
[11] The yacht is named after this figure from Greek mythology
[12] The god of music

Down

[1] Surname of the author that Hilaria plagiarized
[4] Goddess who ate a lot of pomegranates in the underworld
[5] What Professor Ranglefoot is allergic to
[7] First name of the person who gave Professor Ranglefoot the code to Alotta's safe
[8] Food that is in the title of one of Hilaria's books
[9] Location where Hilaria hid the scroll

Answer on page 204

I suggest you take a good look at the evidence you have collected so far. Can you spot any similarities between two of the items? Circle the letters of the two items that share a similar feature.

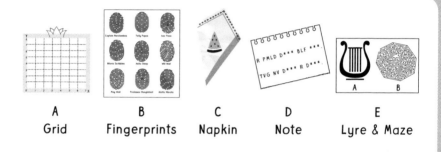

A
Grid

B
Fingerprints

C
Napkin

D
Note

E
Lyre & Maze

Point number	X	Y	
1	ZEUS – POSEIDON	HYPERION – FURIES	
2	HERA – ARES	ARES – ARTEMIS	
3	ARTEMIS ÷ (DEMETER – THANATOS)	(APOLLO – ARES) ÷ (DEIMOS — ERIS)	
4	(DIONYSUS – THANATOS) ÷ (PERSEPHONE – HYPNOS)	(DEMETER – DIONYSUS) ÷ MUSES	

F
Dotted pomegranate

G
Book of gods

H
Pegasus picture

I
Coordinates

HARTIGAN'S HINT: Look at the top of the items. Two have something in common.

Answer on page 205

TASK 10.

What do you know! The grid from Alotta's safe fits perfectly over the spotty pomegranate on the cover of the Greek gods book! If you plot the coordinates you figured out from the god mathematics on pages 114–115, and draw lines so they intersect, you will have a point on the pomegranate.

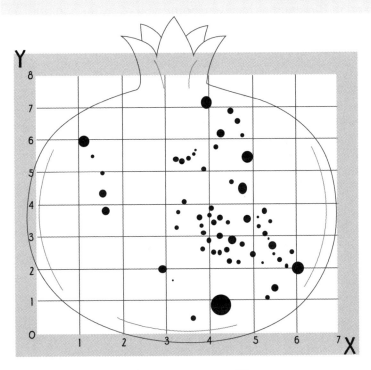

Where do the two lines intersect?
Write the coordinates here: (_____)

 HARTIGAN'S HINT: Draw a line between two opposite points, then draw a line between the remaining two points. They should cross in an X.

Answer on page 205

119

Between the code in the knots and the evidence of Captain Haralambos's interest in *The Pegasus*, it does seem highly likely that he is hoping to buy the scroll from Telly. But you need evidence of this before you can accuse Telly of attacking Ivor and stealing the scroll. Evidence like proof of transfer of money between the two.

It's time to do a little computer hacking! You open the captain's laptop; a quick review of the browser history shows Captain Haralambos has been doing a bit of online banking with Big Bank Greece.

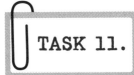

TASK 11.

To unlock the captian's statements, you need to deduce the PIN. Look at the key on the laptop to see which numbers are incorrect, which numbers are correct but in the wrong location in the sequence, and which numbers are correct and in the correct place.

BIG BANK GREECE

9	6	0	3
5	8	6	7
2	1	4	6
4	3	2	2

KEY

☐ NUMBER INCORRECT

☐ CORRECT NUMBER INCORRECT PLACE

■ CORRECT NUMBER CORRECT PLACE

PIN ☐ ☐ ☐ ☐

The PIN is _ _ _ _ .

HARTIGAN'S HINT: Start by looking at the correct numbers in the incorrect places. Can you work out their correct order?

Answer on page 206

You open the transaction files to see:

EVIDENCE LOG 6.

Transaction no.	Payee	Amount in €
501672	T. PAPAS	10,000

Super sleuthing, detective! I do believe you've got him. It's time to confront Telly and tell him that you know he was the one who attacked Ivor Penn and that he has sold the scroll to Captain Haralambos.

You find him on the top deck, serving Alotta, May, and Will some beverages. You clear your throat and make your accusation—and may I say, you deliver your findings with an exquisite blend of calm, authority, and intelligence.

When you have made your case, Alotta and Will both jump to their feet and shout at Telly, "You have my scroll?!"

Alotta looks at Will. "What do you mean *your* scroll?"

"Umm, I meant *your* scroll," Will says, rather unconvincingly.

May covers her face with her hands, and you listen as she says, "Just admit it. The detective will only find out anyway." She's right, of course, you will, but you don't need to employ any of your interrogation techniques because Will spills it all.

"I paid Ivor to track down the lost music for May. I thought *she* should be the one to perform it."

"For May?" Alotta says, turning to her stepsister. "You, sing the lost music from *The Pegasus*?" Alotta laughs. "Oh, darling, I don't think so." Then she turns to Telly. "Now come on, hand over the scroll."

Telly stutters. "I don't have it, I already gave it to Captain Haralambos."

"Well, go and get it back!" Alotta says.

"That is going to be hard to do," Telly says, and points out to sea. "Because that's him on the speedboat."

Well, that is a bit of a setback. "I did make a copy," Telly says, then adds, "and the going price is €10,000."

"You expect me to buy a copy of what is rightfully mine?!" Alotta sputters.

You point out to Telly that he is already going to be facing charges of grievous bodily harm and theft and ask if he really wants to add extortion to that list.

Reluctantly, he pulls out a piece of paper from his back pocket and hands it over.

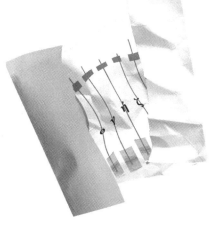

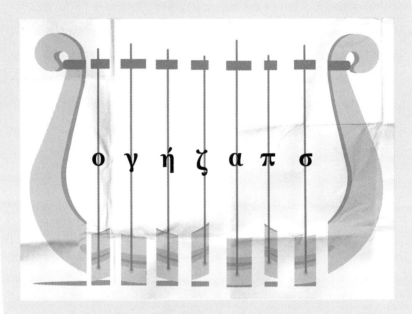

ο γ ή ζ α π σ

Copy of the scroll leading to the missing music of *The Pegasus*

Once you've flattened out the paper a bit, Alotta confirms the copy looks exactly like the original scroll. At first glance, there doesn't seem to be any hint of how it might lead you to the lost music of *The Pegasus*, but I am confident you will discover its secrets in time.

Currently, though, you have a more pressing problem. Captain Haralambos is getting away. You will have to chase after him—so it's full speed ahead into **Case 5: The Captain and the Pomegranate.**

Discoveries so far:

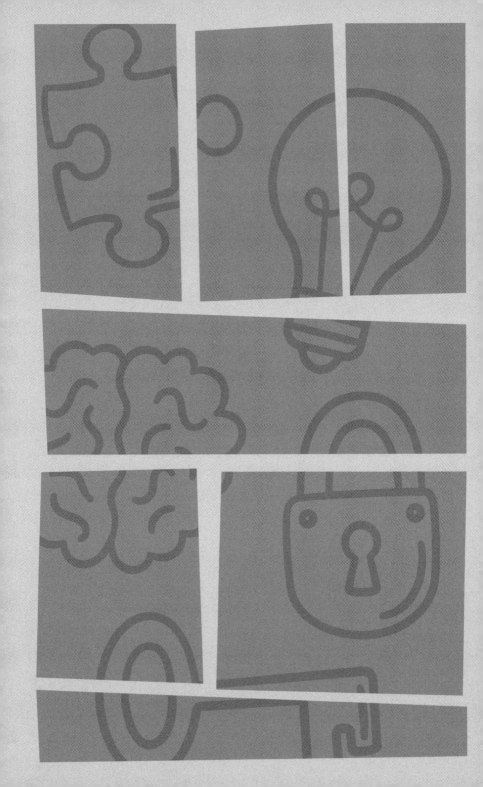

CASE 5:

THE CAPTAIN
AND THE POMEGRANATE

You watch from the side of the *Icarus Infinity* as Captain Haralambos becomes a small dot on the horizon. He must have worked out where the lost music of *The Pegasus* is hidden and set off to retrieve it!

Granted, it is slightly infuriating that he has solved it before you, but do not feel disheartened! You are close, I am certain of that. If only you could figure out what those coordinates were telling you. It is impossible without some kind of map.

A map!

Your mind turns to the maps on the wall in Captain Haralambos's cabin. Of course!

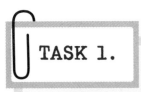

TASK 1.

Look at the maps below and determine which is of interest.

A

B

Write the letter of the map that interests you.

_____

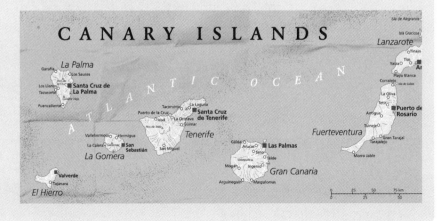

There is something about the position of the islands that is making the cogs in your brain whirl!

You take out the spotty pomegranate grid and hold it up to the map.

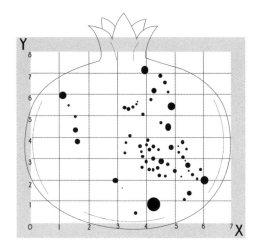

The spots on the pomegranate match up exactly with the location of the islands in the Greek Isles!

TASK 2.

You have determined the coordinates already.

Which island do the coordinates intersect at? _____

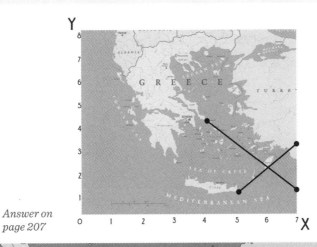

Answer on page 207

TASK 3.

With no captain at the helm, it's going to be up to you to steer the *Icarus Infinity* in the right direction. The *Icarus Infinity* is currently cruising at a bearing of 300 degrees.

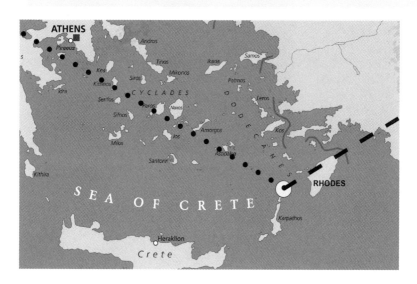

○ *Icarus Infinity*

• • *Icarus Infinity*'s current direction

■ ■ Direction *Icarus Infinity* needs to take to get to Rhodes

 HARTIGAN'S HINT: To work out the angle, count the degrees clockwise from 300° to zero and then from zero to 60°.

The arrow is showing you which angle you need to calculate.

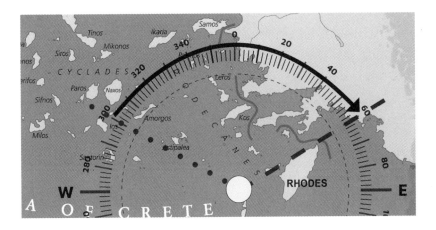

In order to travel at a bearing of 60 degrees to sail to Rhodes, calculate the angle you have to turn the *Icarus Infinity*:

Agent-in-training turned superyacht captain! Very well done—the *Icarus Infinity* is now pointing in the right direction. But you need to increase your speed if you're going to stand a chance of catching up with Captain Haralambos. He's had quite the head start.

Answer on page 208

TASK 4.

To override the cruise control of 18 knots, you need to push the correct button on the control panel. The buttons follow a pattern.

Which button should you select for position 5? Circle the answer.

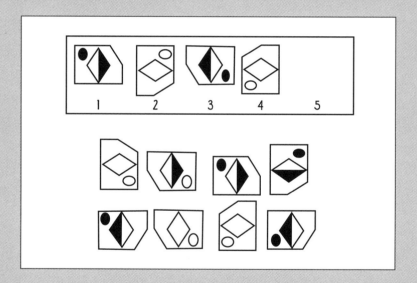

 HARTIGAN'S HINT: Note what angle the buttons turn for each new position. What happens to the oval with each turn?

Answer on page 208

With the *Icarus Infinity* now moving at speed for Rhodes, and with the help of Will Wail who, it turns out, holds a junior license in ship-steering, you set off in pursuit of Captain Haralambos.

Once you arrive at Rhodes, a stressed-out Will hands back the wheel and you make a sterling effort of maneuvering the *Icarus Infinity* into the dock. The bumps don't do any real damage to the *Icarus Infinity*, and I'm sure the owner of the neighboring yacht will simmer down once he's climbed back out of the water.

As you secure the *Icarus Infinity* to the pilings, you spot Captain Haralambos at the port taxi stand. He jumps into a car and speeds off.

You head directly to the taxi office and ask a gentleman, who has a somewhat relaxed approach to customer service, where the car that just left is headed. He says he needs the number of the taxi's parking spot to be able to tell you that.

So off you go, back outside to the taxi stand.

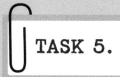

TASK 5.

Using the grid below, determine what number parking spot Captain Haralambos's taxi was in.

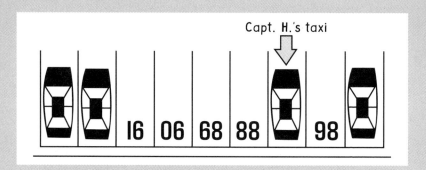

Capt. H.'s taxi

16 | 06 | 68 | 88 | | 98

The taxi was in parking spot number _____.

Back to the office you go with the correct number. Sure enough, the gentleman at the taxi office can track down the location of the captain's car. Once he does, he summons a new taxi to take you in pursuit—to the Acropolis of Rhodes. Like the ancient Greeks, I do love a good Acropolis. Acropolises were fortified areas of a city, built on high ground. In fact, the term *acropolis* comes from the Greek words *akron*, meaning high point, and *polis*, meaning city! Who says you can't learn some interesting facts when you're in the midst of chasing down a criminal captain, hey?!

 HARTIGAN'S HINT: Sometimes it helps to have another point of view. Maybe try looking at things from another direction.

Answer on page 209

Your driver, Mr. Moustakas, seems the cautious type and is unmotivated by your pleas to go a little faster. From the map of Rhodes in the back of the car, you can see that the journey to the Acropolis site on Monte Smith Hill is not long, but it is taking an age to get there. Since we have a few minutes, I can tell you that the last name *Moustakas* means a person with a moustache, which, rather pleasingly, your driver does have!

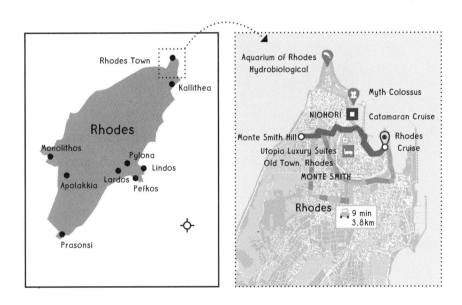

When you finally arrive, there is no sign of the captain. You get out and take in your surroundings, eyes scanning for clues.

You learn that the columns on the ruins in front of you are, in fact, part of the Temple of Apollo, the god of music. This is promising!

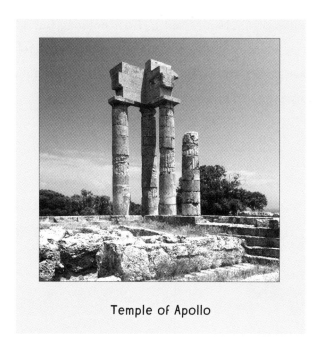

Temple of Apollo

Among the ruins, there is one that grabs your interest: It is a column with the wings of a Pegasus carved out of stone!

Column with wings at the Temple of Apollo

There are two orbs on the wings—perhaps they would once have been coated in gold. Could these be somehow related to the Golden Pomegranate?

The high Greek sun causes the wings to cast a shadow on the ground. You have a feeling the shape it creates is something you have seen before.

What does the shadow remind you of? _____

That's right! It's the shape of the island of Rhodes!

Could the location of the orbs on the shadow-map indicate the location of the lost music from *The Pegasus*?!

TASK 6.

Review the map on page 137.

Where in Rhodes are the Pegasus's wings suggesting you should go?

_____

With the location confirmed, you jump back in the taxi and head for your new destination. There is an acropolis there, too—you are getting quite the cultural tour today!

It is undeniably a spectacular place.

Acropolis of Lindos

Answer on page 209

HARTIGAN'S HINT: Look back at the map from the taxi. Where does the orb line up with on the map?

The Temple of Athena stands atop the hill. A visit to a temple built to honor the goddess of reason, wisdom, and intelligence bodes well for your investigation, don't you think?

As you climb the stairs to the temple and step out high above the Mediterranean Sea, you spot Captain Haralambos in the distance, facing some ruins with his back to you. Then, in front of your eyes, he disappears. One second, he's there, the next, he's vanished! You dash over to the spot where he was standing moments ago, and now there is no trace of him. How very baffling!

You look at the section of the ruins he was facing. On first inspection, you see nothing out of the ordinary, but then you notice that some of the stones protrude slightly. You touch one and find that it can be pushed inward into the wall! Nothing happens, so you try pushing more of the stones, but still nothing comes of it. You take a moment to think. Stepping back, you count sixteen stones that are arranged in groups of four.

Think through the items in your evidence log . . . is there a connection?

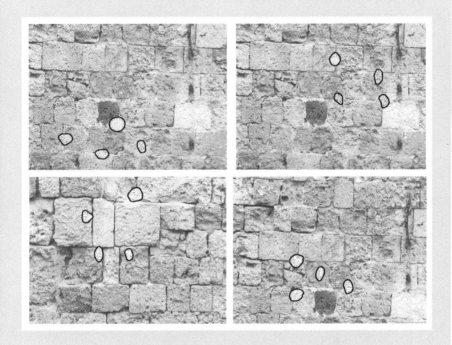

Groups of protruding stones at the Temple of Athena

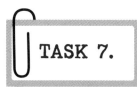

TASK 7.

What do you have that might be relevant to these strange stone patterns?

Circle the letter of the relevant piece of evidence.

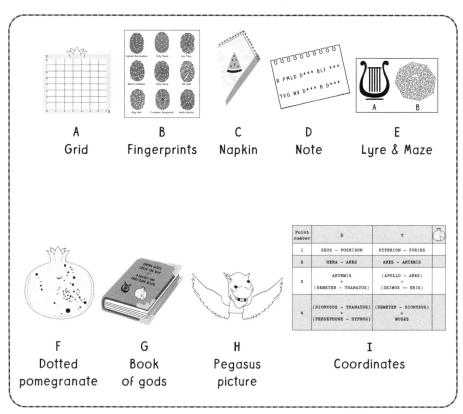

A
Grid

B
Fingerprints

C
Napkin

D
Note

E
Lyre & Maze

F
Dotted
pomegranate

G
Book
of gods

H
Pegasus
picture

I
Coordinates

Yes, your artistic efforts have paid off! It's the Pegasus picture, with the four holes.

Answer on page 210

TASK 8.

Determine which of the stones you need to push inward, by lining up the patterns with the Pegasus's head holes.

Circle the letter of the correct pattern.

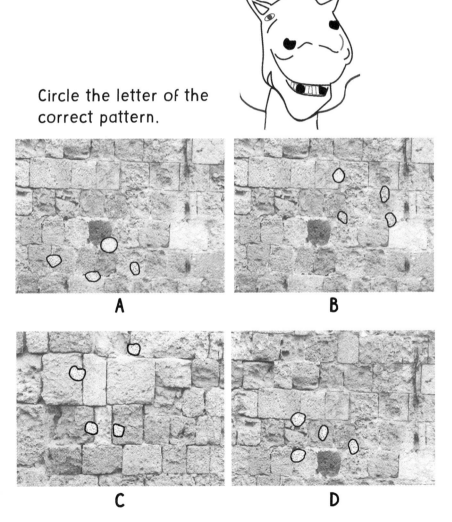

A

B

C

D

When you push the correct four stones in, the floor gives way and you feel yourself sinking. The roof closes over you and it takes a moment for your eyes to adjust to the gloom. You are standing at the top of a stone staircase that leads deep below the Acropolis.

Gracious—what an adventure this is turning out to be! Let's hope that Captain Haralambos, the missing music, and the Golden Pomegranate are under here somewhere. Venture forth, detective, with a sure foot and a clear mind as you continue onward to **Case 6: The Underworld.**

Write your notes and deductions so far:

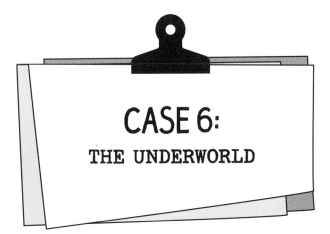

CASE 6:
THE UNDERWORLD

Y ou hurry along a narrow corridor in pursuit of
Captain Haralambos, hoping to catch up with him—
he can't have gotten far! Your way is lit by torches that
are fixed to the wall. The corridor seems to go on forever,
but eventually it opens out into a large circular room.
There are four exits—how will you know which one
to take?

There is a stone pillar in the center of the room.
Something has been carved into the top of it.
You approach the pillar to take a closer look.

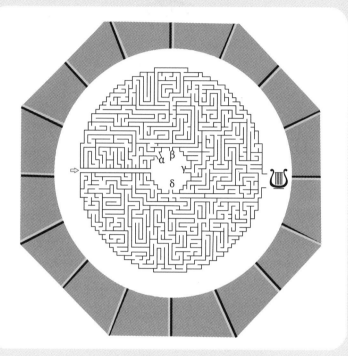

Carving on top of the stone pillar

The carving on top of the pillar shows the corridor that you just walked along and the route that each doorway will lead to.

One of the routes leads to an exit marked with a lyre! Finding that is your goal.

150

TASK 1.

Determine which doorway you should take:
alpha α, beta β, gamma γ, or delta δ.

Circle the Greek letter of the path you need to take. Choose wisely! How terrible if you ended up roaming these passages forevermore!

HARTIGAN'S HINT: It may be easier to start from the lyre and work backward.

Very well done! I did briefly have terrifying visions of needing to advertise for a new recruit because I'd lost you to a secret underground maze in Lindos! Thankfully, you made it through. I wonder how Captain Haralambos fared. I suppose he only has himself to blame if he's gotten lost.

When you step out of the labyrinth of passageways, you find yourself in a vast high-ceilinged chamber. At the opposite end, there are three columns—and a box on top of each of them. A boulder hangs precariously above the third. There is no door that you can see, other than the one you have just come through. You take your first step onto the paved flooring and the tile beneath your foot disappears. You jump back as you watch it dropping into an abyss below. It is several seconds before you hear it smash at the bottom. Clearly, it's a long way down. Tentatively, you nudge another tile with your foot and the same thing happens.

There must be a way to the three columns at the other end of the room that doesn't involve plummeting to your death. You look around and notice another pillar near the entrance you came through. When you take a closer look, you realize that it must be a clue.

Etched on top of the pillar is the Pegasus constellation. Pairs of numbers are carved around the image's circumference.

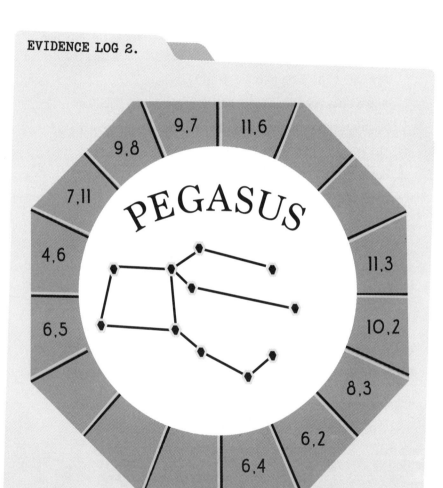

Etching on top of the pillar near the entrance of the room

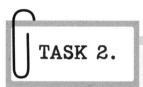

TASK 2.

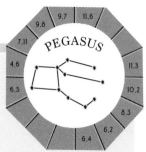

PEGASUS

9,8 | 9,7 | 11,6
7,11
4,6 | 11,3
6,5 | 10,2
8,3
6,2
6,4

Using the pairs of numbers on the Pegasus column, work out which tiles are safe to step on to make your way across the room to the three other columns. The first number tells you which white numbered tile to start at; the second number tells you how many steps to take. Always move in the diagonal direction of the dotted arrow. Draw an ✗ on the stones that are safe to tread on. The first pair of numbers, 6, 5, has been done for you. If you are correct, the ✗'s will make a pattern that matches the stars of the Pegasus constellation.

For example for the first pair of numbers (6, 5): Find the tile with the number 6 on it. Then move 5 spaces diagonally. The ✗ shows you where you will end up.

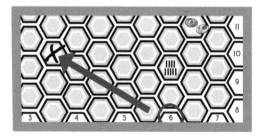

HARTIGAN'S HINT: The tiles' coordinates are the pairs of numbers etched on the pillar surrounding the Pegasus constellation. The first number refers to the number on a white tile. The second number is how many tiles you should count diagonally from the white tile.

Answer on page 212

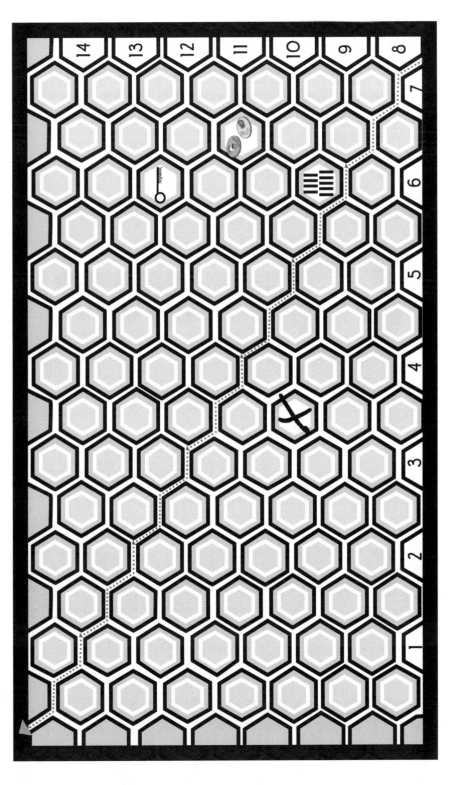

Splendid! (And what a relief!) You have found safe paths to the three columns! You leap across the stones to the three farthest points; each path ends in front of one of the three columns. On the first column you find a key. The teeth are the Greek letters that make up the word *Pegasus*.

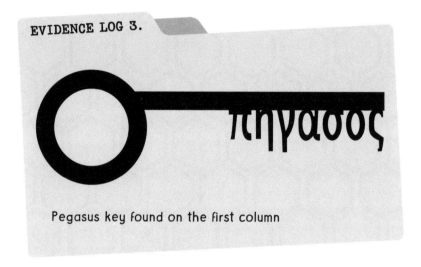

EVIDENCE LOG 3.

πcηγαοος

Pegasus key found on the first column

On the second column, there is a pouch. When you pick it up, it feels heavy, and whatever's within clinks. You tug at the drawstring to look inside and see that the pouch contains gold coins! Lots of them! Oh, that *is* a find!

Gold coins found in the
pouch on the second column

The top of the third column is covered with what appear to be
hundreds of keyholes. The key must fit *one* of them. You could,
of course, try them all, but something tells me that if you select the
incorrect keyhole, the boulder that is hanging over your head may
come crashing down on top of you. Keep a cool head, detective.

TASK 3.

Look at the different keyholes on the right. Find the correct keyhole that fits the Pegasus key that you found on the first column. Once you've identified the correct keyhole, circle it.

Pegasus key found on the first column

 HARTIGAN'S HINT: Try rotating the key 90 degrees counterclockwise to match its teeth with the keyhole patterns.

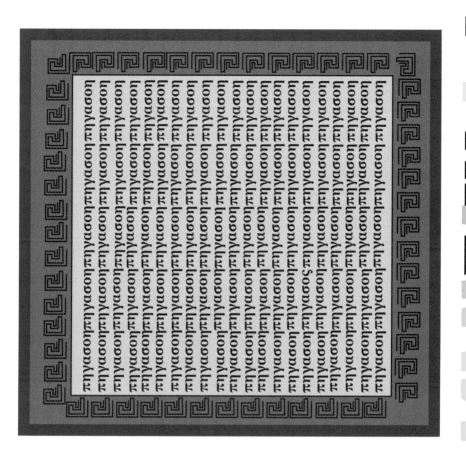

Terrific! I did fear once again for your safety (that you might become too closely acquainted with that boulder), but I should have known you'd find the correct keyhole.

The fact that the key was there at all, and the presence of the coin pouch for that matter, does suggest that Captain Haralambos has not made it this far yet. Perhaps he knows another route, or maybe he is lost in the labyrinth.

Answer on page 213

You put the key into the correct slot and turn. There's a loud clunking noise, and the stone slab you're standing on lowers into the ground. You find yourself in another underground chamber. You're dwarfed by three new columns, each of which seems to be guarded by a statue. In front of them all is an enormous statue of Apollo—the god of music.

EVIDENCE LOG 5.

Statue of Apollo

On the statue is a strategically placed α for Alpha—perhaps it is important?

In his arm, Apollo cradles a lyre.

You note with understandable trepidation that the strings continue upward and attach to some dangerous-looking blades that hang overhead.

The shape of the lyre reminds you of something. You take out the copy of Alotta's scroll that Telly gave you. I do believe that whatever you do here may lead to you finding the missing notes from *The Pegasus*.

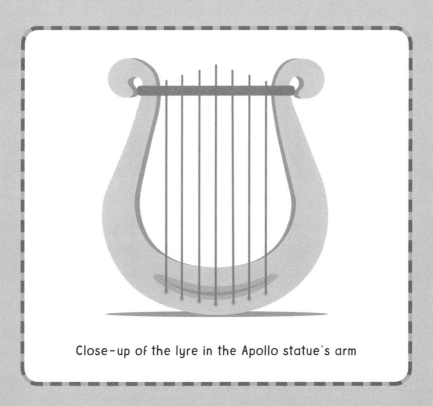

Close-up of the lyre in the Apollo statue's arm

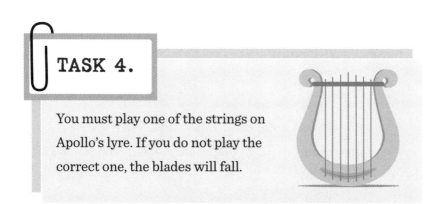

TASK 4.

You must play one of the strings on Apollo's lyre. If you do not play the correct one, the blades will fall.

Arrange the pieces from the copy of Alotta's scroll in the correct order to create an image of a lyre.

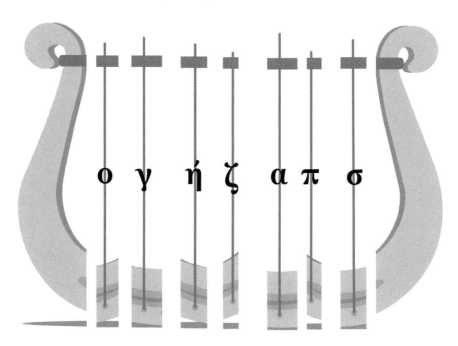

ο γ ή ζ α π σ

 HARTIGAN'S HINT: To help you rearrange the pieces, look at the top and bottom of each piece.

Write the Greek letters in the correct order below:

Excellent unscrambling! The Greek letters spell out the Greek word for *Pegasus*! Now you just have to work out which note to play. Apollo may provide a clue. When you have chosen, circle the Greek letter that corresponds with the correct note.

You pluck the string and the note echoes around the chamber; you look up, mildly concerned that a blade may come hurtling down, but all is still. You needn't have worried—of course you played the correct one!

A whirring sound starts up, Apollo's mouth opens, and out pops a scroll. You lift it from his mouth and unroll it. Inside is a musical score—the missing music from *The Pegasus*! You found it—magnificent! The folks aboard the *Icarus* will be so pleased.

Not one to rest on your laurels, you recognize that your job is not yet finished—you still have a Golden Pomegranate to locate!

As you examine the lost music, you see something that doesn't look quite right: A section of the music does not appear to fit with the rest, and you notice a pomegranate over the clef at the start of the bar.

Answer on page 213

Section of the lost music

You notice that some musical notes are etched into the base of the Apollo statue. It is a key! Each note represents a letter in the Greek alphabet.

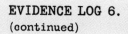

Etching at the base of the Apollo statue

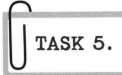

TASK 5.

Use the key to decode the music. Perhaps it will lead to the Golden Pomegranate, as Professor Ranglefoot believed it would!

Write the corresponding Greek letter under each musical note:

____ ____ ____ ____ ____ ____ ____ ____ ____

You have spelled a Greek word, but what does it mean? You scour the chamber and come to a stop in front of the three columns. They, too, have carvings on them.

More Greek letters! Each column has a lever on the side of it. From experience with falling blades and boulders and the like, you imagine that if you turn the wrong one, something bad might happen.

Answer on page 214

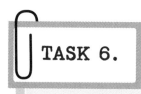

TASK 6.

Use the letters in your Greek word _____ to work out which lever you should pull. Circle the answer.

A

PANACEA

B

π
α
ο
δ ι
ν
σ ι
ε
ώ

POSEIDON

C

π η ό ε
σ
ρ υ φ
ε

PERSEPHONE

Answer on page 214

167

Well done! I knew you'd get the right one. I did think it was probably Persephone since she is partial to the pomegranate, but it's always best that you check properly, especially with the number of booby traps that you've come across.

When you pull the lever, the whole column starts to tip forward. You keep pulling until it is horizontal with the floor and a staircase has been revealed.

You walk down the steps and into another room. This one is much smaller. Inside, on a long stone table, you see some golden weighing scales. In one of the dishes sits a large gold pomegranate. Is it . . . ? It must be! You've found the Golden Pomegranate! You rush over, but as you go to reach for it, you stop yourself, realizing at the last second that it is another trap. In the other dish sits a stone replica of the Pegasus statue.

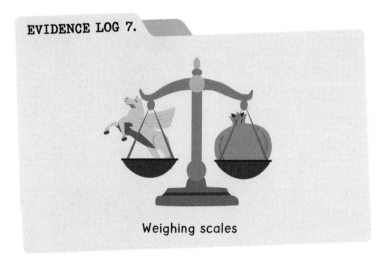

EVIDENCE LOG 7.

Weighing scales

You look around and see there are long slits embedded in each of the walls. Blades glint from the crevices. If you remove the pomegranate, causing the scales to tip, the blades will activate.

To take the Golden Pomegranate, you will need to replace it with something of the exact same weight. But what? A note of guidance, etched into the wall tells you what you need to know.

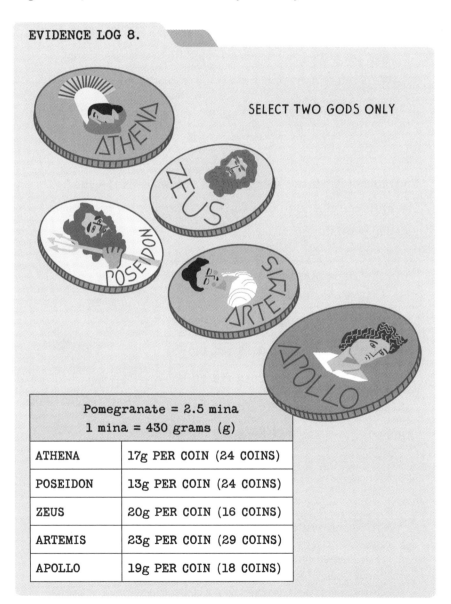

SELECT TWO GODS ONLY

Pomegranate = 2.5 mina
1 mina = 430 grams (g)

ATHENA	17g PER COIN (24 COINS)
POSEIDON	13g PER COIN (24 COINS)
ZEUS	20g PER COIN (16 COINS)
ARTEMIS	23g PER COIN (29 COINS)
APOLLO	19g PER COIN (18 COINS)

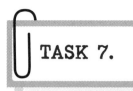

TASK 7.

You understand now! You must use the weight of the coins to replace the Golden Pomegranate in order to keep the scales balanced and avoid further booby traps. Work out which coins you need to replace the Golden Pomegranate.

You must only use two coin types. Of the two gods you choose, you must use all of the coins you have. The number of coins is given in parentheses

Pomegranate = 2.5 mina 1 mina = 430 grams (g)	
ATHENA	17g PER COIN (24 COINS)
POSEIDON	13g PER COIN (24 COINS)
ZEUS	20g PER COIN (16 COINS)
ARTEMIS	23g PER COIN (29 COINS)
APOLLO	19g PER COIN (18 COINS)

SELECT TWO GODS ONLY

HARTIGAN'S HINT: First, work out how much the pomegranate weighs: 2.5 x 430g, or 430 + 430 + 215 (which is half of 430).
Then multiply the weight of each coin by the number of coins you have. E.g., for Zeus, 20 × 16. When you have all the totals, work out which two add together to make the exact weight of the Golden Pomegranate.

170

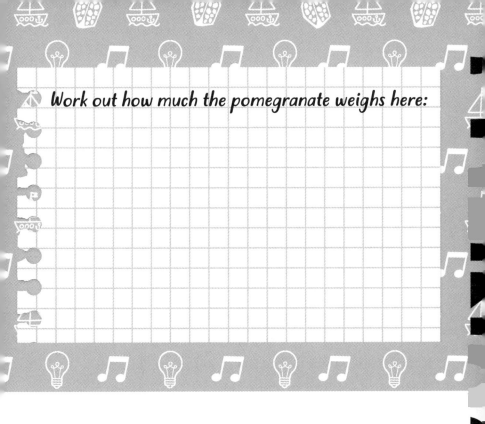

Work out how much the pomegranate weighs here:

The two gods you must choose are:

_____ and _____.

Ever so carefully, you swap the Golden Pomegranate for a handful of coins from the pouch and hold your breath as you wait to see whether it balances.

It does! You can't quite believe it! In your hand is the actual Golden Pomegranate!

I'm afraid to say you don't appear to be any more beauteous yet, but perhaps these things take time.

Answer on page 215

You make for the exit, keen to retrace your steps and get aboveground and into the sunshine, but a figure appears in the doorway. It's Captain Haralambos.

Oh, this is a nuisance. This might not be particularly kindhearted of me, but I had hoped he might have been wandering around the maze for all eternity.

"Thank you," he says, taking a step into the room, "for going to the trouble of finding the Golden Pomegranate for me. I could never have solved those puzzles, but luckily, I didn't have to."

You're about to tell him that after what you've just been through, there's no way you're going to just hand over the Golden Pomegranate, but then you see the harpoon in his raised hand. He takes a step toward you, gesturing for the Golden Pomegranate. You stand your ground, but you'd rather not take your chances against a seasoned sea captain wielding a harpoon. He smiles broadly when you reluctantly hand the Pomegranate over. He hooks his harpoon to the back of his belt, holds up the Pomegranate, and marvels at it. "I have searched a long time for you, my beauty. You will fetch an excellent price."

Ignoring the fact that he's talking to an inanimate object, you tell him that it belongs to the people of Greece. It should be in a museum, where everyone can appreciate it.

"Let them close their eyes and *imagine* a Golden Pomegranate instead! This will make me rich. What purpose would it serve in a glass box for people to file past and glance at?"

You open your mouth to answer, but he continues.

"It does not matter what you think, I have the Pomegranate and that is the end of it." He pauses, taking in the room. His eyes settle on the scales, widening when he spots the gold coins.

"It seems this place has many treasures to offer," he says.

You shout, warning him not to disturb the scales, but he ignores you and reaches for the coins you placed where the Pomegranate used to be. As you predicted, a blade swings from its hiding place in the wall. You launch yourself at the captain to knock him off his feet. The blade misses his head but catches the collar of his shirt. Suddenly, he is airborne—being propelled across the room, arms and legs flailing until he is launched face-first into the stone wall, where his flight ends. The blade comes to an abrupt stop, wedging itself into the stone, pinning him to the wall. The Golden Pomegranate drops from the captain's hand, rolls across the floor, and comes to a halt at your feet.

You pick it up. As you leave to make your way back through the tunnels, you call back, "Looks like you'll be the one having to close your eyes and imagine a Golden Pomegranate now."

Which really is a staggeringly good line. I don't think I could have come up with anything better myself!

But before you get too pleased with yourself, there are a few more loose ends to tie up.

1. Inform the police that they need to come and collect Captain Haralambos. (You didn't wish for him to stay there all of eternity, did you?)

2. Ensure the area is sealed off; you wouldn't want any tourists ruining their vacation by getting lost in that maze or taking a boulder to the head.

3. Deliver the Golden Pomegranate and all the other historical artifacts to a museum.

4. Tell our client, Alotta Vibrato, that you have found the missing music but that she'll have to speak to the museum about whether she can use it.

5. And finally, file a police report letting them know who else needs to be arrested. That list is going to be rather long!

Once you've done all that, I think you have earned yourself an ice cream or two!

Bravo, detective, you conducted a very fine investigation indeed!

List of Criminal Charges

To be filed against:

Professor Archibald Ranglefoot: Theft of one scroll belonging to Alotta Vibrato.

Ms. Anita Sleep: Accomplice to theft of one scroll belonging to Alotta Vibrato.

Ms. Hilaria Scribbles: Poisoning of Professor Archibald Ranglefoot. Theft of one scroll belonging to Alotta Vibrato. Plagiarism of *The Potato* and *There Are Toes on My Feet* by Opus Megalos.

Mr. Ivor Penn: Blackmail and incitement to illegal activity. Theft of one scroll belonging to Alotta Vibrato.

Mr. Telly Papas: Grievous bodily harm. Theft of one scroll belonging to Alotta Vibrato.

Mr. Will Wail: Conspiracy to commit theft of one scroll belonging to Alotta Vibrato.

Ms. May Wail: Accomplice to Will Wail's conspiracy to commit theft of one scroll belonging to Alotta Vibrato.

Captain Haralambos Hondros: Handling stolen goods, including one scroll belonging to Alotta Vibrato. Possession of an unregistered weapon. Threatening with said unregistered weapon.

THE
DAILY WAIL

GOLDEN POMEGRANATE
MIGHT NOT BE THAT GOLDEN

The Golden Pomegranate, which hit the news following its discovery in hidden tunnels under the Acropolis of Rhodes, has become the subject of debate following a spate of accidents that have befallen museum staff.

The Pomegranate, according to myth, was thought to bring its owner gifts such as beauty, love, marriage, hope, prosperity, and eternal life, but has so far failed to deliver on any of these claims.

Concerns have been expressed that the Pomegranate may, in fact, be cursed. These allegations started after several staff and members of the public were hospitalized following the Pomegranate's arrival at the museum.

In fact, minutes after its installation, the Pomegranate fell from its stand, knocking cleaner Nikos Ioannous unconscious. In rushing to Ioannous's aid, security guard Elena Giorgiou then proceeded to fall unconscious as well, after tripping and headbutting a nearby display cabinet. The cabinet, containing ancient Greek weaponry, crashed to the floor, and a javelin was somehow propelled forward, embedding itself into the buttocks of museum guide Lucas Demetriou. Understandably shocked, Demetriou leapt forward and caused a display pedestal to topple over.

Subsequently, a large amphora with a depiction of a battle scene from the Trojan War was sent rolling across the floor, sending two museum visitors "flying like bowling pins."

The amphora continued down the main staircase, picking up speed, and exited the building through the front doors, where it caused passerby Hector Booras to take evasive action. Unfortunately for Booras, he swerved his mobility vehicle into recently dug roadwork pits. It took one crane and several firefighters two hours to remove Booras and his scooter from the hole.

Christina Sotir, the museum curator, has denied that these improbable accidents are associated with the Golden Pomegranate. Speaking from her hospital bed, after being electrocuted in an incident which "is definitely not related to the Pomegranate," Sotir says that the public can visit the museum's newest artifact with confidence.

MINI SUDOKU
PLACE NUMBERS 1–6 IN EACH
3 × 2 BLOCK, COLUMN, AND ROW.

2		1	6		4
4		3	5	2	
	3		1	4	
	2	4			
6		2	4		3
3				1	6

Answer on page 217

WORLD HAS ALOTTA SAY ABOUT VIBRATO'S COMEBACK

Celebrated soprano Alotta Vibrato returned to the stage after a fifteen-year hiatus to perform *The Pegasus* in its entirety.

Unfortunately, the world will have to wait a little longer to hear the missing opera music because Ms. Vibrato was forced to end the performance prematurely following an unexpected and explosive stomach incident, which occurred while she was attempting to reach a high A. While there has been no official comment, a source close to Alotta put this unfortunate accident down to the singer's consumption of an undercooked octopus.

Perhaps, though, her early departure was a blessing, as the reaction to Alotta's voice has not been one of unbridled positivity.

While some critics have described Alotta's new sound as "courageously experimental," "interestingly discordant," and "challengingly novel," others have been more brutal in their assessment, with one reviewer stating, "I believe my ears are quite traumatized," and another saying, "We should all send thanks to that octopus."

Alotta has confirmed that she will return to the stage, saying that she promised the late composer, Sascha van Tootahonk, that she would gift the missing music to the world, and she is determined to deliver on that promise.

Let's hope that's all she delivers.

WEEKLY WORD FINDER

There are some words hidden in the following sentences. Can you find them?

(E.g. "In a poll of the public, 90% stated that Alotta's swift exit from the stage was the most memorable performance in all operas to this day." The word Apollo is hidden across three words: A POLL OF.)

Words to find: Lyre, Gold, Athena, Icarus.

1. Alotta Vibrato has happily received an invitation to London's Royal Opera House.

2. She will sing old hits as well as the missing music from *The Pegasus*.

3. Alotta, the natural choice to perform the missing music according to some critics, will perform for one week only.

4. Alotta says that the performance will be "energetic, a rushing melody of heaven-sent notes."

A MEGA LOT OF SCRIBBLES

In news that has shocked the literary world, Hilaria Scribbles and Opus Megalos, the author she plagiarized, are teaming up to coauthor two novels, *Vegetable Soup* and *Together We Have Twenty Toes*. These books will examine the significance of root vegetables and feet and will contain "philosophical explorations into the importance of forgiveness and moving on from our mistakes."

Scribbles, affectionately known as the Poisoned Pen after lacing Professor Archibald Ranglefoot's milkshake with egg, will be writing her contributions to the books from prison.

> **Editor's Note:** Following the arrest of journalist Ivor Penn and owner Will Wail, today's edition of *The Daily Wail* has been written and edited by May Wail.

ANSWERS

ANSWERS:
AGENT SELECTION

TASK 1.
From page 2

From page 3.

To find patterns, first align all the numbers.

8	1	2	3
2	1	8	3
5	3	2	8

From this, you can see the number 1 appears twice in position two. This means that it must be the letter **O**.

8	1 = O	2	3
2	1 = O	8	3
5	3	2	8

Now look at the numbers in position four and see the number 3 appears twice. When looking at your three starter words, you can see that the number 3 could be either T or E. You can deduce it must be E because both NOTE and TONE have the number 1 in the second position.

8	1 = O	2	3 = E
2	1 = O	8	3 = E
5	3 = E	2	8

There is only one word with 3/E in the second position, so you know it must be **PENT**.

8	1 = O	2	8 = T
2	1 = O	8	3 = E
5 = P	3 = E	2 = N	3 = T

8	1	2	3
T	O	N	E
2	1	8	3
N	O	T	E
5	3	2	8
P	E	N	T

You can now fill in the remaining numbers and determine that OPEN is:

1532

PASSCODE

TASK 2.
From page 6

To work out the **X** coordinate: 8 − 3 = 5, and 5 + 1 = 6

To work out the **Y** coordinate: 9 ÷ 3 = 3

X	Y
$(\eta - \gamma) + \alpha$ $(8 - 3) + 1$	$\dfrac{\theta}{\gamma}$ or $\theta \div \gamma$ $\dfrac{9}{3}$ or $9 \div 3$

The coordinates of (6,3) reveal the location of the *Icarus Infinity* is Greece.

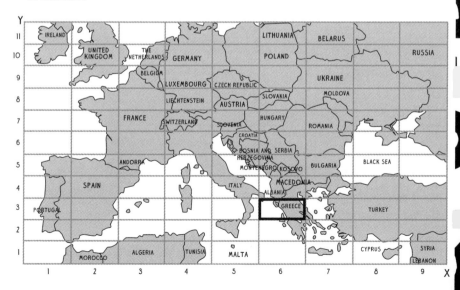

TASK 3.

From page 8

Each arrow rotates clockwise by 45 degrees.

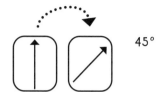

45°

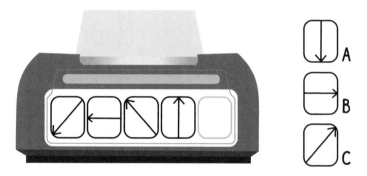

A

B

C

The correct arrow is button **C**.

From page 10.
The flight number is **3223**.

TASK 1.
From page 14

The code you were asked to remember is your flight number: **3223**.

From the starting position, move three spaces to the right, two spaces up, two spaces to the left, and three spaces up.

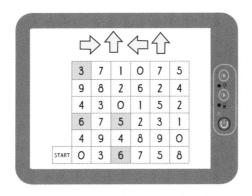

The shaded numbers in the tablet above reveal the numbers you land on after each step. In order, the numbers create the four-digit code: **6563**.

TASK 2.
From page 20

The missing numbers are **64** and **32**.
The four-digit PIN is:

TASK 3.
From page 22

I	C	A	R	U	S	B	D	E	F	G	H	J
A	B	C	D	E	F	G	H	I	J	K	L	M

K	L	M	N	O	P	Q	T	V	W	X	Y	Z
N	O	P	Q	R	S	T	U	V	W	X	Y	Z

Name	First 4 Letters	Code
ALOTTA VIBRATO	ALOT	IHLQ
CAPTAIN HARALAMBOS HONDROS (HARA)	HARA	DIOI
TELLY PAPAS	TELL	QUHH
IVOR PENN	IVOR	EVLO
PROFESSOR ARCHIBALD RANGLEFOOT (ARCH)	ARCH	IOAD
HILARIA SCRIBBLES	HILA	DEHI
ANITA SLEEP	ANIT	IKEQ
MAY WAIL	MAYW	JIYW
WILL WAIL	WILL	WEHH

TASK 4.

From page 24

Time	Codes	Suspects	Time	Codes	Suspects	Time	Codes	Suspects
4:30 P.M.	IHLQ IKEQ QUHH	ALOTTA ANITA TELLY	6:15 P.M.	IOAD DEHI	PROF. RANG. HILARIA	8:00 P.M.	DEHI	HILARIA
4:45 P.M.	IOAD	PROF. RANG.	6:30 P.M.	JIYW	MAY	8:15 P.M.	IOAD QUHH	PROF. RANG. TELLY
5:00 P.M.	IHLQ QUHH	ALOTTA TELLY	6:45 P.M.	WEHH	WILL	8:30 P.M.		
5:15 P.M.	EVLO	IVOR	7:00 P.M.	QUHH IKEQ	TELLY ANITA	8:45 P.M.	IHLQ	ALOTTA
5:30 P.M.	JIYW	MAY	7:15 P.M.			9:00 P.M.	IKEQ	ANITA
5:45 P.M.	DIOI QUHH	CAPT. HARA. TELLY	7:30 P.M.	IKEQ	ANITA			
6:00 P.M.	QUHH IKEQ	TELLY ANITA	7:45 P.M.					

The suspects are those who were in the corridor after Alotta put the scroll back at 7:00 p.m. The suspects in the corridor between 7:15 p.m. and 9:00 p.m. are:

Telly Papas

Anita Sleep

Hilaria Scribbles

Professor Archibald Ranglefoot

TASK 5.

From page 32

From top to bottom, left to right, the code reads: **6432**.

1	3	5	6	4	2
4	2	6	5	3	1
5	6	2	4	1	3
3	4	1	2	6	5
2	1	4	3	5	6
6	5	3	1	2	4

6432 is the same four-digit code that unlocks Alotta's safe (page 20)!

TASK 6.
From page 35

FINGERPRINT A   FINGERPRINT B

ANITA SLEEP   PROFESSOR RANGLEFOOT

TASK 7.
From page 38

Professor Ranglefoot dropped the watermelon napkin. With his fingerprints on the paper and the fact that he was in the corridor, you have caught him red-handed!

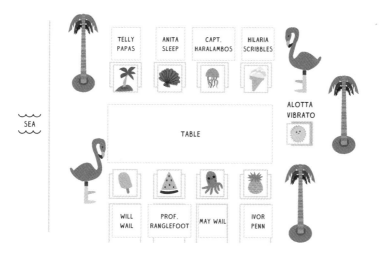

Do you remember what the professor is allergic to? **Eggs**

ANSWERS:
CASE 2: THE PROFESSOR'S POISONER

From page 44

Anita Sleep left her fingerprints on the note.

TASK 1.
From page 46

R
I

P	M	L	D
K	N	O	W

D	*	*	*
W	*	*	*

B	L	F
Y	O	U

*	*	*
*	*	*

.

T	V	G
G	E	T

N	V
M	E

D	*	*	*
W	*	*	*

R
I

D	*	*	*
W	*	*	*

.

TASK 2.
From page 52

Letters collected:

χρυσός

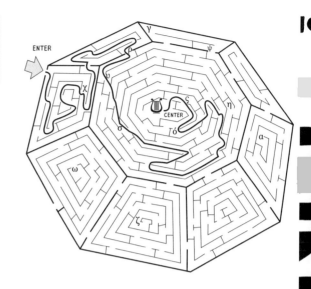

TASK 3.
From page 54

Letters collected:

ρόδι

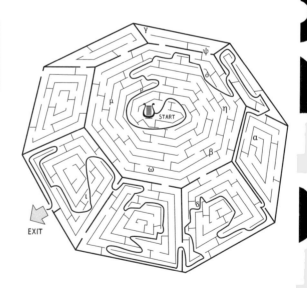

TASK 4.
From page 56

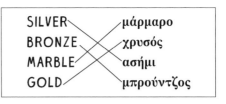

SILVER	μάρμαρο
BRONZE	χρυσός
MARBLE	ασήμι
GOLD	μπρούντζος

Marble starts with **Mu** μ. So the word would be **μάρμαρο** or **μπρούντζος**. *Gold* includes **Rho** ρ so it could be three of them. We know it can't be **ασήμι**. *Bronze* includes **Pi** π so it has to be **μπρούντζος**. *Silver* and *marble* contain **Alpha** α so they could be **μάρμαρο** or **ασήμι**. The first word is **GOLD**.

TASK 5.
From page 58

The second word is **POMEGRANATE**.

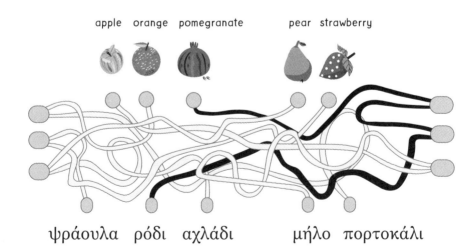

apple   orange   pomegranate   pear   strawberry

ψράουλα   ρόδι   αχλάδι   μήλο   πορτοκάλι

Suspect	Calculations	Time in seconds
CAPT. H.	(Bridge to stairs) 25s + (Stairs × 3) 45s + (Stairs to Prof. R.'s cabin) 20s	90
IVOR and WILL	(Start to first staircase) 5s + (Stairs × 3) 45s + (Stern stairs to middle stairs on owner's deck) 10s + (Stairs to Prof. R.'s cabin) 20s	80
TELLY	(Stairs × 2) 30s + (Stern stairs to middle stairs on owner's deck) 10s + (Stairs to Prof. R.'s cabin) 20s	60
HILARIA	(Stairs × 2) 30s + (Stairs to Prof. R.'s cabin) 20s	50
ANITA	(Stern stairs to middle on owner's deck) 10s + (Stairs × 1) 15s + (Stairs to Prof. R.'s cabin) 20s	45
MAY	(Start position to stairs on bottom deck) 15s + (Stairs to Prof. R.'s cabin) 20s	35

You can eliminate anyone who would take over one minute (60 seconds) to reach Prof. R.'s cabin, so the suspects are now **Telly**, **Hilaria**, **Anita**, and **May**.

TASK 7.
From page 66

	RED	BROWN	WHITE	GRAY	TRIANGLE	SQUARE	DIAMOND	CIRCLE
ANITA	✗	✓	✗	✗	✗	✓	✗	✗
MAY	✗	✗	✓	✗	✗	✗	✓	✗
HILARIA	✓	✗	✗	✗	✓	✗	✗	✗
TELLY	✗	✗	✗	✓	✗	✗	✗	✓
TRIANGLE	✓	✗	✗	✗				
SQUARE	✗	✓	✗	✗				
DIAMOND	✗	✗	✓	✗				
CIRCLE	✗	✗	✗	✓				

Name	Suitcase description
ANITA	BROWN, SQUARE LOGO
MAY	WHITE, DIAMOND LOGO
HILARIA	RED, TRIANGLE LOGO
TELLY	GRAY, CIRCLE LOGO

TASK 8.
From page 68

The suitcase containing the eggs was **red** and had a **triangle logo**.
It belongs to **Hilaria Scribbles**.

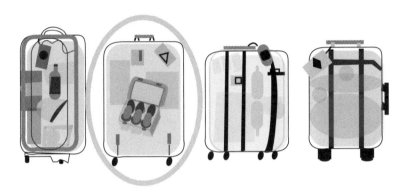

TASK 9.
From page 71

R PMLD DSZG BLF WRW.
I KNOW WHAT YOU DID.

TVG NV DSZG R DZMG.
GET ME WHAT I WANT.

ANSWERS:
CASE 3: THE TOILET TANK BLACKMAILER

TASK 1.
From page 78

Key N opens the locked briefcase. (Rotate the shape beneath the key 90 degrees clockwise to match the lock shape.)

TASK 2.
From page 80

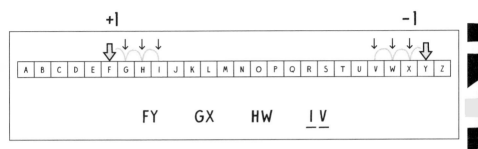

+1   −1

A B C D E F G H I J K L M N O P Q R S T U V W X Y Z

FY   GX   HW   <u>I V</u>

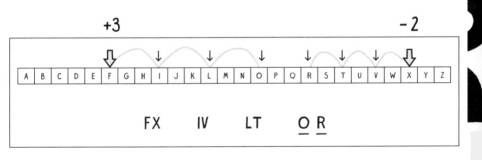

+3   −2

A B C D E F G H I J K L M N O P Q R S T U V W X Y Z

FX   IV   LT   <u>O R</u>

I-V-O-R. Ivor's password is his *name*!

TASK 3.

From page 82

𐅇 = 5000

𐅅 = 500

Δ = 10

Γ = 5

||| = 3

Total = 5,518

a) 𐅇 𐅅 Δ Γ ||| = 5,518

X = 1000

X = 1000

X = 1000

H = 100

H = 100

𐅄 = 50

ΔΔ = 20

|| = 2

Total = 3,272

b) XXXHH𐅄ΔΔ|| = 3,272

ANSWERS:
CASE 4: WHY CAN YOU NEVER FIND A PENN WHEN YOU NEED ONE?

TASK 1.
From page 94

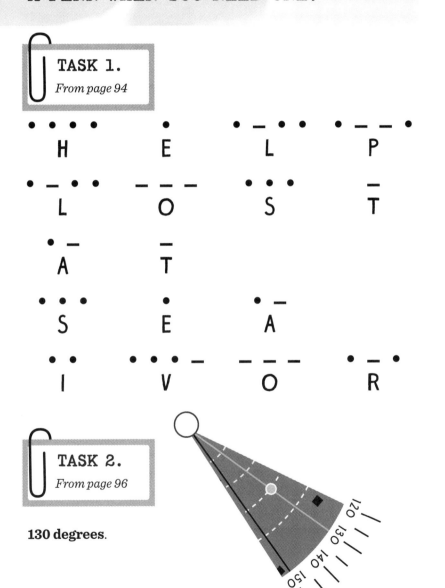

H E L P
L O S T
A T
S E A
I V O R

TASK 2.
From page 96

130 degrees.

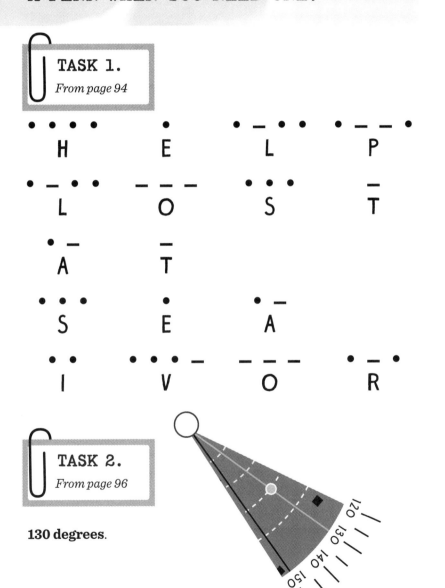

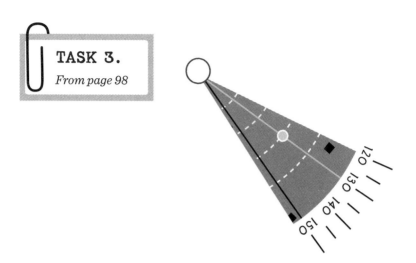

TASK 3.

From page 98

Each radar line represents 15 knots, so 3 × 15 knots = 45 knots.

$$\underset{\text{Distance}}{\text{45 knots}} \div \underset{\text{speed}}{\text{15 kph}} = \underset{\text{time taken}}{\text{3 hours}}$$

$$\underset{\text{time now}}{5\text{:}30} - \underset{\text{time taken}}{\text{3 hours}} = \underset{\text{time Ivor went into the water}}{\text{2:30 p.m.}}$$

From page 100

The three suspects without an alibi are: **Will Wail, Captain Haralambos, Telly Papas**

TASK 4.
From page 103

Your prime suspect is the person who was in possession of the bronze bust: **Telly Papas**.

		Suspect			Location		
		CAPTAIN HARALAMBOS	WILL WAIL	TELLY PAPAS	BOTTOM DECK	OWNER'S DECK	MAIN DECK
Object	👤	✗	✗	✓	✓	✗	✗
	🧯	✓	✗	✗	✗	✗	✓
	🐒	✗	✓	✗	✗	✓	✗
Location	BOTTOM DECK	✗	✗	✓			
	OWNER'S DECK	✗	✓	✗			
	MAIN DECK	✓	✗	✗			

TASK 5.
From page 105

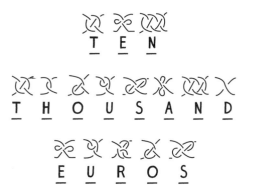

T E N

T H O U S A N D

E U R O S

3		8			2			5	8
6		1	0	4	5	3		4	
4	4	7		2		6		2	
9				3	4	2		5	
		9		5		1	4	8	6
8	3	0	7	6			0		2
1		5		7			3		2
9	8	5				2	1	7	3
4			6	1	4		1		
1	5	3	8		0		8	4	6

The number that doesn't fit in the grid is **7812**.

Point number	X	Answers	Y	Answers	Coordinates
1	ZEUS – POSEIDON	100 – 95 = 5	HYPERION – FURIES	64 – 63 = 1	(5,1)
2	HERA – ARES	90 – 83 = 7	ARES – ARTEMIS	83 – 80 = 3	(7,3)
3	ARTEMIS ÷ (DEMETER – THANATOS)	68 – 48 = 20 80 ÷ 20 = 4	(APOLLO – ARES) + (DEIMOS – ERIS)	86 – 83 = 3 + 38 – 37 = 1 3 + 1 = 4	(4,4)
4	(DIONYSUS – THANATOS) + (PERSEPHONE – HYPNOS)	54 – 48 = 6 45 – 44 = 1 6 + 1 = 7	(DEMETER – DIONYSUS) ÷ MUSES	68 – 54 = 14 + 14 ÷ 14 = 1	(7,1)

TASK 8.
From page 116

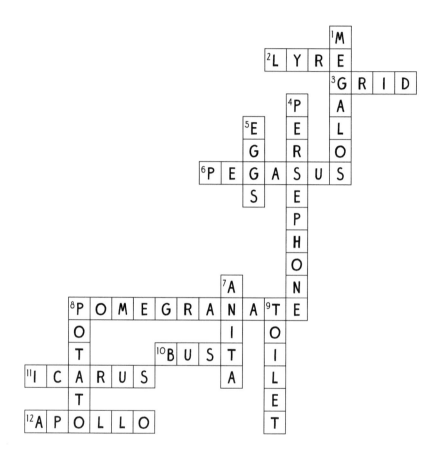

```
                              ¹M
                          ²L Y R E
                              E  ³G R I D
                              ⁴P   A
                          ⁵E  E   L
                          G  R   O
                      ⁶P E G A S U S
                          S  E   S
                              P
                              H
                              O
                  ⁷A       N
              ⁸P O M E G R A N A ⁹T E
              O           I   O
              T      ¹⁰B U S T  I
          ¹¹I C A R U S    A   L
              T          A   E
          ¹²A P O L L O       T
```

TASK 9.
From page 118

The grid has the same crown as the spotted pomegranate.

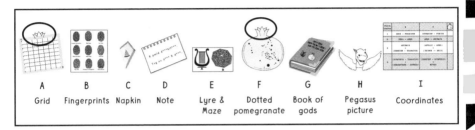

A	B	C	D	E	F	G	H	I
Grid	Fingerprints	Napkin	Note	Lyre & Maze	Dotted pomegranate	Book of gods	Pegasus picture	Coordinates

TASK 10.
From page 119

The god coordinates intersect at **(6,2)**.

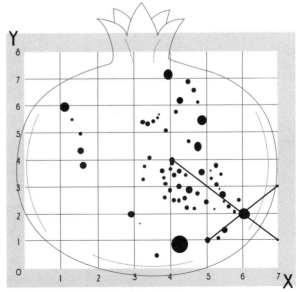

We know that the dark gray 2 is the correct number in the correct location in the sequence. So the fourth digit is 2.

Looking at the pale gray numbers (the correct numbers in the incorrect places), there are three numbers: 1, 4, and 6.

You can see that the 4 is in the incorrect position when it's first or third, so it has to be in the second position.

$$\_ \ 4 \ \_ \ 2$$

Then looking at the remaining two numbers (1 and 6), you can see that the 6 is in the incorrect position when it's third, so it has to be first.

$$6 \ 4 \ \_ \ 2$$

So we know that the 1 has to be in the third position.

The correct order is **6412**.

ANSWERS:
CASE 5: THE CAPTAIN AND
THE POMEGRANATE

TASK 1.
From page 128

Map **A** is a map of the Greek Isles.

(A)

TASK 2.
From page 131

The island is **Rhodes**.

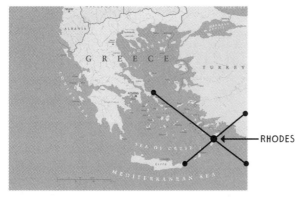

RHODES

TASK 3.
From page 133

The angle between a bearing of 300 degrees and a bearing of 60 degrees is 120 degrees.

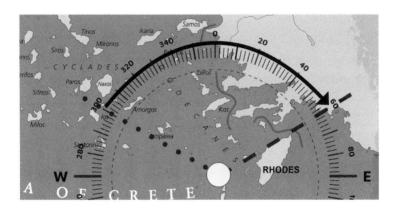

TASK 4.
From page 134

The button rotates 90 degrees clockwise each time. The oval changes from black to white with each new turn.

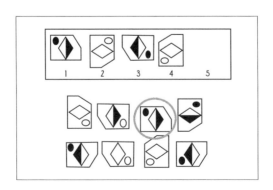

TASK 5.
From page 136

From the angle that you approach, the parking spot numbers are upside down. If you flip them over, the parking bay numbers go up by increments of 1.

85	86	87	88	89	90	91	92	93

TASK 6.
From page 141

The wings look like the map of Rhodes. The placement of the gold orb matches up with the placement of Lindos on the map, suggesting that you should go to **Lindos**.

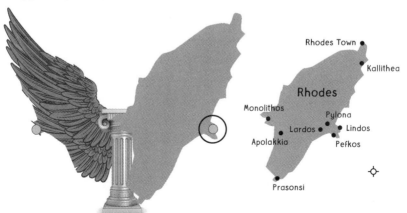

TASK 7.
From page 144

A
Grid

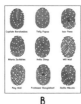

B
Fingerprints

C
Napkin

D
Note

E
Lyre & Maze

F
Dotted
pomegranate

G
Book
of gods

H
Pegasus
picture

I
Coordinates

TASK 8.
From page 145

The correct pattern is **C**.

C

TASK 1.
From page 151

The exit you should take is delta δ.

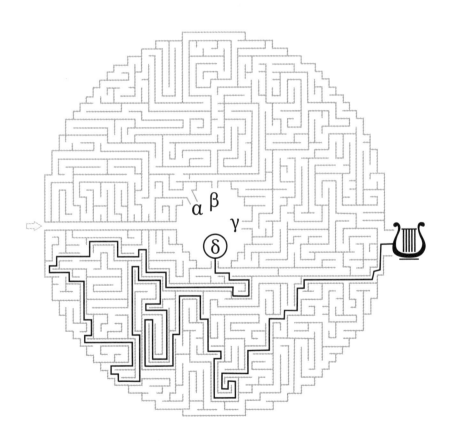

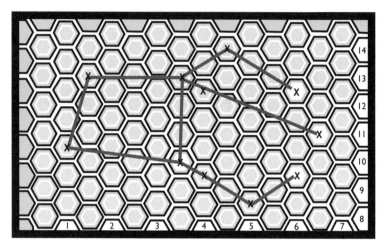

6, 5 = Find the number 6 and count 5 tiles diagonally from it.

4, 6 = Find the number 4 and count 6 tiles diagonally from it.

7, 11 = Find the number 7 and count 11 tiles diagonally from it.

9, 8 = Find the number 9 and count 8 tiles diagonally from it.

9, 7 = Find the number 9 and count 7 tiles diagonally from it.

11, 6 = Find the number 11 and count 6 tiles diagonally from it.

11, 3 = Find the number 11 and count 3 tiles diagonally from it.

10, 2 = Find the number 10 and count 2 tiles diagonally from it.

8, 3 = Find the number 8 and count 3 tiles diagonally from it.

6, 2 = Find the number 6 and count 2 tiles diagonally from it.

6, 4 = Find the number 6 and count 4 tiles diagonally from it.

TASK 3.
From page 159

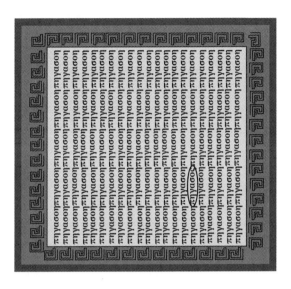

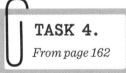

TASK 4.
From page 162

The correct order of the
strings appears on the right.
According to the strategically
placed letter on the Apollo
statue, you should pluck the
string labeled with the letter
α.

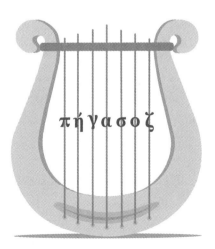

π ή γ α σ ο ζ

π ε ρ σ ε φ ο υ η

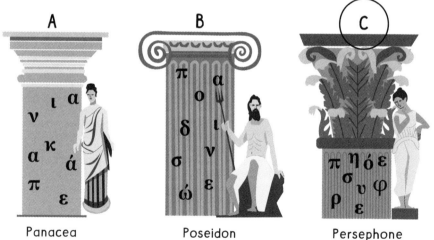

A — Panacea

B — Poseidon

C — Persephone

πανάκεια	ποσειδώνα	περσεφόυη
Panacea	Poseidon	Persephone

The musical score spells out **P-E-R-S-E-P-H-O-N-E**.

TASK 7.
From page 170

Athena and **Artemis** will balance the scales.

Pomegranate = 2.5 mina 1 mina = 430 grams (g)		430 × 2.5 = 1,075g
ATHENA	17g PER COIN (24 COINS)	17 × 24 = 408g
POSEIDON	13g PER COIN (24 COINS)	13 × 24 = 312g
ZEUS	20g PER COIN (16 COINS)	20 × 16 = 320g
ARTEMIS	23g PER COIN (29 COINS)	23 × 29 = 667g
APOLLO	19g PER COIN (18 COINS)	19 × 18 = 342g

408 + 667 = 1,075g
ATHENA & ARTEMIS

The Golden Pomegranate weighs 2.5 mina, and 1 mina = 430g.

So 430g × 2.5 will give you the weight of the Golden Pomegranate.
430 × 2.5 = 1,075g

Each Athena coin weighs 17g and there are 24 of them, so the total weight of all the Athena coins can be found with the equation:
17 × 24 = 408g.

Each Poseidon coin weighs 13g and there are 24 of them, so the total weight of all the Poseidon coins can be found with the equation:
13 x 24 = 312g.

Each Zeus coin weighs 20g and there are 16 of them, so the total weight of all the Zeus coins can be found with the equation: $20 \times 16 = 320g$.

Each Artemis coin weighs 23g and there are 29 of them, so the total weight of all the Artemis coins can be found with the equation: $23 \times 29 = 667g$.

Each Apollo coin weighs 19g and there are 18 of them, so the total weight of all the Apollo coins can be found with the equation: $19 \times 18 = 342g$.

Now you need to work out which two sets of coins will add up to the total weight required to balance out the Golden Pomegranate (1,075g).

Looking at the total weight of each set of coins, you know that the sum of their last digits needs to be a 5. So if you start with 408 (the total weight of the Athena coins), you can see that 408 + 667 (the total weight of the Artemis coins) will end in a 5, since $8 + 7 = 15$.

408 + 667 = 1,075g

ANSWERS:
THE DAILY WAIL

From pages 176 and 177

Mini Sudoku:

2	5	1	6	3	4
4	6	3	5	2	1
5	3	6	1	4	2
1	2	4	3	6	5
6	1	2	4	5	3
3	4	5	2	1	6

Weekly Word Finder:

1. Alotta Vibrato has happi**ly re**ceived an invitation to London's Royal Opera House. **Lyre**

2. She will sin**g old** hits as well as the missing music from *The Pegasus.* **Gold**

3. Alott**a, the na**tural choice to perform the missing music according to some critics, will perform for one week only. **Athena**

4. Alotta says that the performance will be "energet**ic, a rus**hing melody of heaven-sent notes." **Icarus**

CONGRATULATIONS!

Well done, detective! Your instincts prevailed, and you've proven yourself a reliable investigator yet again. I'm always in need of a clever young mind to help with my caseload, so please pour yourself a mug of hot chocolate and join me for *Cluedle: The Case of Rudolph's Revenge* (available Fall 2025).